INNER SEARCH

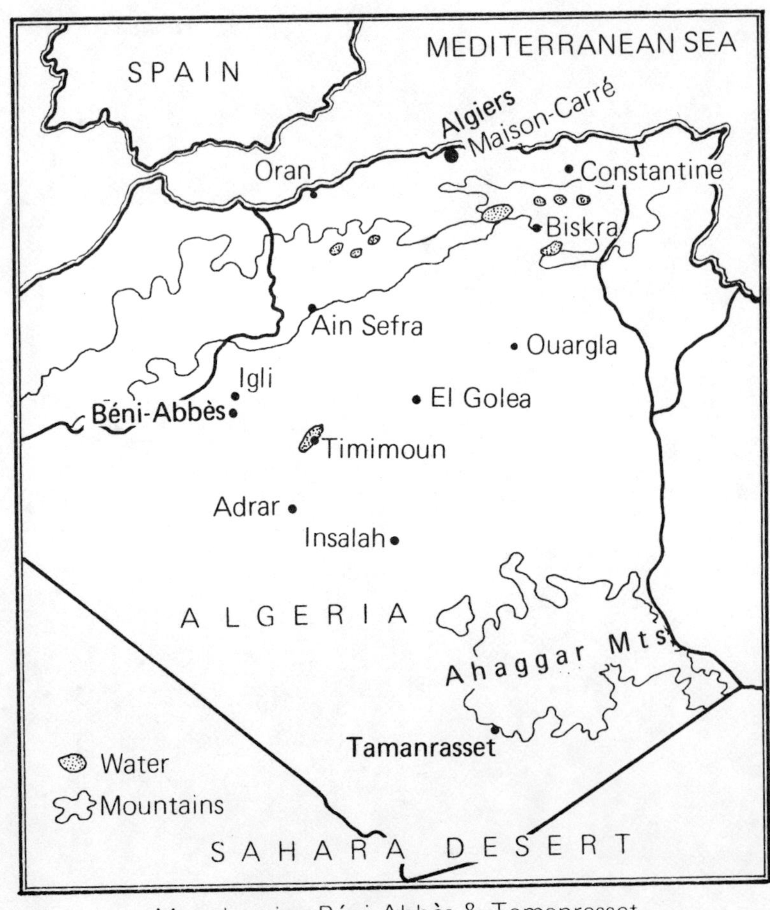

Map showing Béni-Abbès & Tamanrasset

Inner Search

Letters (1889–1916)

Charles de Foucauld

Translated by Barbara Lucas

Maryknoll, New York 10545

1979

The Catholic Foreign Mission Society of America (Maryknoll) recruits and trains people for overseas missionary service. Through Orbis Books Maryknoll aims to foster the international dialogue that is essential to mission. The books published, however, reflect the opinions of their authors and are not meant to represent the official position of the society.

Library of Congress Cataloging in Publication Data

Foucauld, Charles Eugène, vicomte de, 1858-1916.
Inner search.
Abridged translation of the author's Lettres à mes frères de la Trappe published in 1969.
First published in English in 1977 under title: Letters from the desert.
Includes index.
1. Foucauld, Charles Eugène, vicomte de, 1858-1916. 2. Trappists—Algeria—Correspondence.
I. Title.
BX4705.F65A413 1979 217'.125'024 79-4353
ISBN 0-88344-281-7

First published in Great Britain in 1977 by Burns & Oates Limited, 2-10 Jerdan Place, London SW6 5PT

Published originally in French under the title *Lettres à mes Frères de la Trappe* by Editions du Cerf, Paris, France, copyright © Editions du Cerf

U.S. Edition, 1979, Orbis Books, Maryknoll, NY 10545

Printed and bound in the United States of America

Contents

Foreword

Charles de Foucauld was a great letter-writer and much of his correspondence has already been published, whether in the many biographies of him that have been written or in specific volumes of his letters. It was not, however, until the late 1960s that the monks at the Trappist monastery of Notre-Dame des Neiges (Our Lady of the Snows), where Charles de Foucauld started his life as a religious, edited and presented for publication his letters to his Trappist brothers which are preserved in that monastery's archives. Unfortunately the collection is incomplete. Not all his letters were kept by their recipients, not all found their way to the archives. For those that survive we are indebted to Dom Martin de Gonzague, abbot of Notre-Dame des Neiges from 1887 to 1908, and an inveterate keeper, filer and curator.

The French edition of these letters came out in 1969, admirably presented and introduced by Frs A. Robert and Jean-François Six. It contains much incidental material that throws light on Charles de Foucauld in his Trappist context - notably letters from him to other people (not Trappists) and from diverse correspondents, Trappist or otherwise, that concern him and are also in the archives; it also gives biographical accounts of the brothers who played an important part in his life whether or not he wrote to them. These addenda have been greatly abbreviated in the English edition, and there are some omissions even in the letters themselves, but as most of the omitted material is repeated elsewhere nothing is lost of the writer's extraordinary personality.

There is no need to give any account of Charles de Foucauld's life from 1890, when he became a Trappist, until 1916, when he was assassinated, for its broad outline is sketched in the pages that follow. But a few dates are provided as signposts to his life before 1890 for the benefit of those readers who are meeting him for the first time.

A few dates

15 September 1858	Birth at Strasbourg.
1860	Birth of his sister and only sibling.
1864	Death of their father and mother; they go to live with their maternal grandfather, a retired colonel.
1870	The family's removal to Nancy after the defeat of France and the annexation of Alsace in the Franco-Prussian war. Charles attends the lycée.
28 April 1872	Confirmation and first Communion.
August 1874	Passes his Baccalauréat, part I; examiner's comment 'fairly good' (assez bien).
August 1875	Passes his Baccalauréat, part II; same comment.
October 1875	Unhappy, disturbed; is sent away from school.
1876	Enters the military school, St-Cyr (82nd out of 412 candidates in the entrance examination.)
1878	Death of his grandfather is a great blow to him.
1878/9	Enters the cavalry school at Saumur. His inclinations to greed, self-indulgence and dissipation become very marked, helped by a large inherited legacy and rich pleasure-loving friends.
1880	Departure with his regiment to Algeria. Is put on half pay due to his laziness and dissolute life. Rallies when his regiment is involved in a campaign in south Oran and distinguishes himself.

1882	Resigns from the army for fear that garrison life again with not enough to do will undermine his newly-found morale.
1882/4	After intensive preparation makes exploratory journeys into hitherto uncharted areas of Morocco.
1886	Publication of his important work: *Reconnaissance au Maroc*. Encounter with Abbé Huvelin. Conversion.
1889	Vocation to the religious life.

I
Letters from a postulant (1889-1890)

In 1889 Charles de Foucauld, then aged 31, made four retreats to discover with what religious order his vocation lay. After a ten-day retreat at the Trappist monastery of Notre-Dame des Neiges, in the Ardèche department of France, and after consultation with Abbé Huvelin (a priest well-known in religious circles in Paris at that time for his spiritual guidance), he decided to enter there, so embarked on a brief and very formal correspondence with the novice-master, Fr Eugène.

Paris,
4 November 1889 *(to Fr Eugène)*

Reverend Father: I am making so bold as to write to you, following the permission you very kindly gave me. First of all I must thank you for the great charity you showed me when I was at Notre-Dame des Neiges, for your goodness to me, your care of me and loving trust in me; if it is my duty to love all the Lord's children with my whole soul, then how specially devoted must I be to you who did everything to inspire my tender gratitude.

I want to tell you about myself, Father, and I feel that this is what you yourself would like. My inclinations still draw me to be a child of St Bernard; indeed if I follow the feelings which I am sure are inspired by God's mercy, I find that your Order is the one that enables the Christian life to be lived most fully, the life of total union with our Lord. Union with our Lord means sharing all his feelings, living his life; it means loving God above everything and loving his children to distraction, it means living through sacrifice; and it seems to me that the love and sacrifice by which God lived are the two things by which St Bernard also lived and by which you try to live, and you want your sacrifices to be the same as our Lord's in that you passionately want to share his poverty and the humbleness of his work. That is the life to which my own desires draw me, the life through which it seems to me that our Lord is consoled and glorified as much as he possibly can be by men. But am I being pushed in this direction by *his* spirit? Is it in this particular way that *he* wishes me to put myself at his feet? I think a few weeks' waiting will enable us to know. That is what Abbé Huvelin thinks - he wants me to stay in Paris a little longer, just a few weeks, in the tranquillity that my very withdrawn life here grants me, consulting the Lord, asking him for the grace to know his will and to do it. Do join us in praying to him, Reverend Father; ask him particularly to get me out of myself, to love myself only for him; ask him for my needs while asking him for the needs of all his other children, and I beseech you above all to ask him to bring about his heart's desires in the souls that are especially dear to me.

And with this prayer I shall leave you, Father. I shall let you know just as soon as things become clear, because I believe you are with me at the feet of the Lord, and I feel close to you when I am in front of him. I am very far from forgetting you.

Please be good enough, Reverend Father, to accept the expression of deepest gratitude from your very humble, devoted and grateful servant,

Ch. de Foucauld

Paris, 50 rue Miroménil,
30 November 1889 (*to Fr Eugène*)

Reverend Father: I was most touched by your letter and most grateful for it. I beg you to convey my gratitude to

Reverend Father Abbot for the lines he so kindly added to yours.

The reason why I have not written before to thank you for the charity you showed me in your letter, Father, is that I felt and hoped that I would soon know what was God's will regarding me, and I did not want to write without being able to tell you something definite.

But now he has deigned in his mercy to let me know his will in a very positive way through the voice of my spiritual director, a voice which is His,[1] and conforms to all the advice I have been given and all the inclinations of my heart. So I am writing on behalf of Abbé Huvelin to ask you, to beg you, to find out whether Reverend Father Abbot would agree to accept me at Notre-Dame des Neiges. If the answer is in the affirmative I shall arrive before New Year's Day in the hope of doing my novitiate with you, a period to be determined by my superiors and yourself, and then going on to Notre-Dame du Sacré-Coeur[2] if this is, as I belive it to be, the blessed will of our Father who is in heaven. I beg you, Reverend Father, to write and give me all the information I need, tell me whether you can receive me towards New Year's Day and let me know everything I should do before placing myself at your feet and receiving your blessing and that of the Reverend Father Abbot.

I commend myself to your prayers, Father, more than ever. You must be aware of my need to grow in faithfulness, gratitude, strength and love! This will be a difficult month, my last among those I love, so I beg you to pray for me; but I ask you with all the strength of my heart, and all the fervour I possess, and all the charity you may feel towards me, to pray much more for the souls that are dearest to me, the souls whose material presence I am about to leave, pray as much as possible for them, pray as much as God's charity will inspire you I beseech you, and pray a little for me, but much more for them.

Please convey to Reverend Father Abbot the religious respect and devotion of one who hopes soon to be his son, and please accept the expression of the deepest respect and gratitude of your very humble and devoted servant,

Ch. de Foucauld

Dijon,
14 December 1889 *(to Fr Eugène)*

Reverend Father: Your letter has arrived and I have read it with joy and gratitude; I thank God for it, and you too.

As you are allowing me to come among you to follow our Lord, I shall come soon. However, I shall not be with you for Christmas, at least not in body; Abbé Huvelin, who has read your letter, has told me to stay on in Paris until the New Year, so I plan to arrive at Notre-Dame des Neiges in early January; I shall let you know the date as soon as it has been decided by my spiritual director.

I am in Dijon at the moment saying goodbye to my sister. I return to Paris on the 20th and shall not leave it again until I come to you.

Thank you, Father, for your prayers; they have sustained me and will, I hope, help me more and more; and thank you especially for praying for those who are dearest to me, I commend them to your prayers more and more.

Very soon, Father, I shall be with you at our Lord's feet, meanwhile I do not forget you and we are already together at his feet in truth. Please give me your blessing, and give it to those I hold in my heart. . . Allow me to express the respectful devotion and religious gratitude of your very humble servant,

Ch. de Foucauld

Paris,
28 December 1889 *(to Fr Eugène)*

Reverend Father: I am writing to inform you that unless I hear from you to the contrary I shall arrive at

Notre-Dame des Neiges on Tuesday, 7 January. I shall leave Paris on the evening of the previous day, the 6th. On Monday the 6th, Father, please pray to our Lord Jesus that I may receive and retain in my heart all the sentiments he would like to see there on that day, pray him that his will may be accomplished in me on that great day, and pray him still more that the will of his heart may be fully accomplished in all his children, but especially in those that he has given me very particularly to love.

May I ask you that three masses for three special intentions be said at Notre-Dame des Neiges on 6 January and three more on the 7th.

I kneel at your feet, Father, and at the feet of Reverend Father Abbot, to receive your blessing for me and mine; I can already call myself your child, and I pray God to grant you all the graces that he came to the earth to bring, and shower them on you with the abundance his heart would wish. Your very respectful, devoted and humble servant and son in our Lord,

Ch. de Foucauld

Paris,
2 January 1890 *(to Fr Eugène)*

Reverend Father: Abbé Huvelin has instructed me to let you know that I shall arrive at Notre-Dame des Neiges on 16 January instead of the 7th. My spiritual director told me this morning that he is postponing my departure for nine days because of the cold. So I shall leave Paris on the 15th instead of the 6th. I hope, Reverend Father, that you will not forget me in your prayers during these days of waiting, so that this delay ordained by God may be employed according to his holy will, and so that my last days spent among those dearest to me may be given to glorifying him better than heretofore; it is a time of preparation that the Lord has arranged for me, a time of recollection and adoration. Pray that I may spend these days in a holier way than the preceding ones, in detachment from myself and attachment to him. Pray too, I beg you, for those whom I love more than myself.

In addition to the masses that I made so bold as to ask you to say on 6 and 7 January, may I ask you to say six others, three on the 15th and three on the 16th, all for special intentions.

I kneel at your feet and ask you for a blessing for my loved ones and myself. Your very devoted, respectful, grateful and humble servant and son in Our Lord,

Ch. de Foucauld

II
The novice and the young professed monk: letters from Akbès (1890-1893)

Charles de Foucauld, having taken the habit and been re-named Br Marie Albéric, left Notre-Dame des Neiges on 26 June 1890, arrived at Alexandretta, Syria, on 9 July and reached Notre-Dame du Sacré-Coeur on the 11th. This Trappist foundation at Akbès, which depended from Notre-Dame des Neiges, dated only from 1882 so was still very young when Charles de Foucauld arrived there; it consisted mainly of huts and make-shift buildings – hence the pioneering nature of some of the manual labour and the seeming difficulty of achieving a 'regular' life, i.e., a life according to the Rule. The prior of Notre-Dame du Sacré-Coeur (who was in fact away when Charles de Foucauld arrived there) was Dom Louis de Gonzague, brother of the abbot of Notre-Dame des Neiges, Dom Martin de Gonzague, to whom, as well as to Fr Eugène, the following series of letters is addressed.

The Trappist monastery of Notre-Dame du Sacré-Coeur,
by Alexandretta (Syria)
14 July 1890 *(to Dom Martin)*

Very Reverend Father: How much I have to thank you for, for all that you have meant to me at Notre-Dame des Neiges and especially for your kindness in accompanying me to Marseilles! That journey in your company, and that last mass which I served at Notre-Dame de la Garde, were very lovely for me and make my great debt to you even greater. And then at Notre-Dame des Neiges we never dare knock at your door when we want to - although it's always open - because you're so busy, whereas I spent more than twenty-four hours with you and enjoyed your presence for longer in that space of time than we normally do over months. I need hardly tell you how moved I was to part from you, because I feel you have shown more than forbearance towards me, more than kindness, rather a very tender and attentive charity; you have certainly been an abbot - 'Abba' - to me in the true sense of the word; how could my heart not have felt the separation keenly? Your goodbye at the station is still with me and I'm sure it always will be.

What is there to say about my journey? Not very much. Thanks to you it all went marvellously. I couldn't have been made more welcome wherever I landed. The sea was excellent and I wasn't ill; I heard holy mass at the Piraeus (where a missionary who knew the city showed me the way) and at Salonica and Smyrna. I didn't land at Mercina where holy mass must already have been said when I arrived. At Alexandretta I found Fr Etienne who had come to meet me and we arrived at Notre-Dame du Sacré-Coeur on Friday evening the 11th. I was received with the greatest kindness by Dom Polycarpe[1] and here I am in this new community which beats with the same heart as N.D. des Neiges, and I am full of admiration for all that these good fathers have achieved in such a short time, faced with so many difficulties and in this climate. There are four of us novices here, I hope many more will come and that this daughter of N.D. des Neiges, born of such labour, may grow quickly and become more and more beautiful in the eyes of her Father who is in heaven.

What else shall I tell you? That I have found many things to console me in what I have seen here these last few days. And I shall ask you to pray for me because this new departure has been a real sacrifice and I have great need of prayers, but please pray infinitely more for my intentions, for those children I told you about whom I love much more than myself, and for their parents to whom I owe so much and from whom I have received so much. To pray for my intentions is the great charity I ask of you, you who have so much charity towards me.

As for me, I am nothing, yet I on my side pray God for you every day. May he repay you the good you have done me as only his heart knows how, and may he give you what his love wants to give you; this is the prayer of your very humble servant and son in Our Lord,

Br Marie Albéric

The Trappist monastery of Notre-Dame du Sacré-Coeur, by Alexandretta (Syria)
14 July 1890 *(to Fr Eugène)*

Reverend Father: I am very grateful to Dom Polycarpe for allowing me to write to you, indeed telling me to do so. I have little to report about recent happenings as my journey passed without incident, but a whole lot to say about the past, about my happiness in being under your direction, having you as novice-master, and my sorrow at leaving you – You were the first person to welcome me to N.D. des Neiges, you gave me so many hours of your time and did me so much good, you were so kind, so forbearing, so fatherly towards me and so often had to endure my many failings! Were I to try to thank you for all you meant to me, for all you did for me, it would take a long time as I would have to retrace day by day the five and a half months I spent at N.D. des Neiges. Dear Notre-Dame des Neiges, where I received the sacred habit, where God gave me so many graces, where he sustained me so well, both soul and body, where I became so keenly aware of how totally we are in his hands, and of the gentleness of his hands, and of the loving care with which he carries us along! I shall never see it again, at least I hope not - as you know I don't want to be a travelling monk - but I shall often be there in my thoughts, indeed I often am there when I pray to our Lord for those who are worth much more than me, the prayer of the sinner for the just, such a prayer is madness, I know, but God is so good that I can risk this madness! It is impossible and pointless to try to describe the kindness with which Dom Polycarpe has welcomed me here - you know him and can guess; he is my novice-master and the superior until the return of the prior. There are four of us novices, one who has been here for some time, a priest from France who has been here for two or three months, and a Maronite priest, a postulant, who arrived a few days ago; and there are also three lay-brother novices.

Everything is encouraging; it is obvious that God is helping. Pray for me, you know how much I need your prayers, and don't forget those whom I have commended to your prayers, give them a share of your thoughts and your prayers and you will do me the charity I desire. As for you, you will never lack a sinner's prayers; I can never forget my father in our Lord; wretched as I am, I am your respectful, devoted and grateful son,

Br Marie Albéric

The Trappist monastery of N.D. du Sacré-Coeur, by Alexandretta (Syria)
16 September 1890 *(to Dom Martin)*

Reverend Father: I was just starting to write to you this morning when your letter of 25 August arrived - thank you very much and thank you for all your kindness and affection. Though you don't like being thanked you must allow me to tell you how happy and touched I am that you went to see Madame de Bondy.[2] She was delighted with your visit and very grateful. Thank you!

I am distressed by what you tell me about Father Eugène's health; letters take so long to get here that I hope he may be better by now; I am enclosing a note for him and one for dear Br Norbert. I pray for you every day, Reverend Father, it is the very least I can do. But what are my prayers? Thank you for your constant ones for me. I rejoice with you for the temporal favour God has granted you; I rejoice equally that he has given you a good novice; how I would love to see that dormitory and refectory full of good monks - it cut me to the quick to see them so empty! I hope the young Kabyle will do well, what a blessing, a soul thus won over to God.

Thank you for your advice and for what you say about

love for the rule, '*Si diligis me, serva mandata*'; that's what I like to hear, there lies the truth which brings everything to the love of God. I shall try to follow you, Reverend Father, never forget to urge me on.

You ask me to tell you about myself and I shall do so in a way that will console you. I am in immense peace, God is sustaining both my body and soul, I praise him every day for having brought me here. My life is exactly what it was at N.D. des Neiges, I don't think I have changed very much. It will hardly surprise you to hear that Dom Polycarpe's spiritual direction suits me admirably, he has planned me as regular a life as it is possible to have here, I myself find it regular (except on one point which is not his responsibility, the refectory). For the work period he has put me with a brother postulant, a young and very edifying Maronite priest, under the supervision of Fr Philomène; thus regular communal work is never lacking, we work in the fields, sometimes in the laundry, it's very good. In short I praise God for having brought me here, I praise him for the time I spent at N.D. des Neiges, I praise him for having brought me here, I am in immense peace under Dom Polycarpe's direction. My soul was cowardly and listless when I first arrived, but God thought me too weak to be left in that state and has restored my peace to me. I think I am very much as I was at N.D. des Neiges - just one external difference - I take a midday siesta.

I shall give your message to good Fr Philomène. His example and that of Dom Polycarpe are strengthening and consoling. Thank you for asking him to pray for me. That is just like you.

With profound respect, Reverend Father, and deepest gratitude, I am your very humble and devoted servant and son in our Lord,

Br Marie Albéric

P.S. Fr Philomène asks me to give you his greetings from a loving heart and to thank you for your message; he promises to pray for you and me.

JMJB[3] *The Trappist monastery of N.D. du Sacré-Coeur, by Alexandretta (Syria)*
15 November 1890 *(to Dom Martin)*

Reverend Father: Four months have already passed; following your permission[4] I am writing to ask your blessing and to talk to you a little. About myself? There's not a great deal to say: God keeps me in the same health and the same peace; he sustains me here just as he sustained me at N.D. des Neiges. About my life? It is regular except for the food, which is sad; indeed Dom Polycarpe has given me as regular a life as is possible, even more regular than at N.D. des Neiges thanks to the regular work under the supervision of Fr Philomène; you, however, have deprived me of this salutary work for a while now and given me work which I'm incapable of doing, the laying out of paths.[5] Luckily Br Joseph is better at this work than me and with his help it is going ahead. Once it's finished I would like never to go out of the convent again. I hope it will not be too grand when it's finally built; if my plans are accepted the building shouldn't be too expensive. But I would like a huge enclosure, thick and high. I have often envied our Trappist sisters.

About my soul? I am very cowardly and lukewarm. Outwardly I'm just as you knew me, but inwardly I'm becoming more and more cowardly and lukewarm, avoiding all hardship and effort, all that is not pleasing to nature.

Perhaps you are wondering whether I'm happy to have come to N.D. du Sacré-Coeur? Yes, I thank God for it every day, indeed my whole letter must make you sense my conviction that here I am in the place to which I was called. I can only be thankful with my whole soul for this infinite grace and be faithful to it. But you must never imagine that I forget N.D. des Neiges or that I do not often feel close to you and Fr Eugène; one does not forget the place where one received the sacred habit, the nuptial habit; if profession is true marriage, then taking the habit is that too to a lesser degree, it is at least a betrothal to which both heart and soul are totally committed. And then both you and Fr Eugène were so good to me, all the fathers and brothers of N.D. des Neiges showed me such touching charity! I often look back on myself in the solitude of the enclosure and the novice-house in the snow and cold of last winter and remember how I blessed the snow and cold for bringing so much silence.

My letter was interrupted at that point, Reverend Father, and I'm delighted it was because a few hours later yours of 18 October arrived. Thank you a thousand times for writing, need I say what a great and true consolation your letters are to me.

You ask how I practise the rule. The same as at N.D. des Neiges; but perhaps I no longer have the same horror of breaking the silence, I have even spoken two or three times without permission - pray for me about this. The work is very regular. The intervals are spent in church or the novice-house; I am learning some psalms, I read the holy Bible though not very much because in summer the intervals are short; I pray, more by words than by thoughts, alas! I sleep in the dormitory, that is very regular; I had a midday siesta while the summer exercises lasted.

Divine Office is very consoling, it is said with great reverence and edification thanks to Dom Polycarpe who attends and leads all the offices; I am glad to be able to tell you this as you will be consoled by my description.

I cannot leave you, Reverend Father, without sending you my wishes for your feast day; you can imagine how close I felt to you on St Martin's day, and I asked this dear and admirable saint to make good my prayers for you and draw you closer to him and to God every day of your life and in heaven. If I, bad as I am, pray for you and never forget you, how much more must he pray for you, he who was so charitable on earth and now burns with the fire of eternal Love to which he is so close! The thought consoles me.

Please accept, Reverend Father, the deep, respectful and grateful devotion of your son in our Lord,

Br Marie Albéric

JMJB N.D. du Sacré-Coeur,
17 January 1891 *(to Fr Eugène)*

Dear and venerated Father: it was a year ago yesterday that you welcomed me at N.D. des Neiges, I see you still rather unwell in your cell; it was a year ago today that I entered the community, and a year ago the day before yesterday that I said my goodbyes on earth to all I love best in this world; the 26th was the grace of the sacred habit, the dates come crowding thick and fast, it is a period full of emotion, full of graces, may it be full of gratitude and love! May our Lord Jesus put in my heart what he wishes to be there and make me receive it well, may he make me faithful to such generosity, faithful to consoling his heart, faithful to forgetting myself and thinking only of consoling that! How sweet it is for me that I chose these days to thank you for your welcome letter of 13 December and for your new year wishes and for all you have been to me during the year that has just finished, the first of my religious life. Thank you, Father, with my whole heart, my thanks are not much but I express them with the consolation that our heavenly Father will repay you a hundredfold (and think of his hundredfold!) for the good you have done me. It is a gentle thought which carries me far from this sad earth into a blessed region where we shall, I hope, love and adore for all eternity our Lord Jesus and the holy, blessed, ever-serene Trinity!

You ask what I think about obedience in matters of judgement. I haven't really given it a thought since leaving N.D. des Neiges. I think you must have prayed for me not to be tempted in that direction and your prayers have been answered. I have been utterly at peace; if once or twice the devil and nature have tried to tempt me God has swiftly driven them away through the help of St Theresa who told her nuns to look on their superiors, in everything, as our Lord himself. My soul abides in a growing peace, it has pleased God to increase this peace even more since I came here; and he sustains my body in the same perfect health.

Thank you for your good news about Madame de Bondy, thank you for not forgetting my intentions in your prayers, it is very sweet for me, it is the greatest charity you could do me, thank you. I on my side do not forget you and yours...

I like Fr Prior very much, he is very, very good, the first at all the offices, devoted to the rule. Dear Fr Polycarpe has influenza but is a little better now. I hope you are getting better too. When you write tell me about your health, it is important to me.

May our Lord look after you throughout the new year, dearest and most venerated Father, and may he draw you closer and closer to him in this world until it pleases him to do so in the next. Your respectful and very affectionate son in our Lord,

Br Marie Albéric

JMJB N.D. du Sacré-Coeur,
Friday 10 April 1891 *(to Fr Eugène)*

Dearest and most venerated Father: Now that Easter is over I can rejoice in talking to you about it and consoling myself for the long silence of Lent, a blessed silence and a precious period of recollection that our letters would not have disturbed had we been able to write to each other, as we speak only of God, and yet I have to admit that at certain times silence is even better.

I hope you are well, Father, and that this hard winter hasn't tried you too much; I hope you have consolations, that God is giving you good novices and work that conforms to the cherished abjection that we have come to seek. I am well, my soul and body are as you knew them, the same perfect health, the same peace. I read little, indeed I read nothing, because manual labour takes up a lot of time and the short intervals are given to prayer or letters, small occupations, visits to superiors, and so on, and most of all to being in church.

I find regular work suits me very well, it is good for the soul, it is poverty, abjection, mortification, obedience, prayer, it would be an admirable time for prayer if I were more faithful, less careless, less dissipated. May God give me what I lack, I lack everything, may he give me humility above all - humility, repentence, horror for my sins and esteem for my neighbour, ask him to give me these, commend my dearest intentions to him, you know what they are; I do not forget you and yours.

I receive holy communion as often as at N.D. des Neiges, it is an infinite blessing. Fr Polycarpe is everything that you predicted he would be for me, and Fr Prior is very very kind, but those who are present do not make one forget the absent, you know, and the love that comes from God isn't like human love, these don't drive out those, they all enter the heart together and give each other mutual help so as ceaselessly to grow, for surely they must grow so as to be able little by little from within this sad world to echo the charity of the elect in heaven. May our hearts love, love much and quickly, and make us so sad on this poor earth that God will deliver us out of pity and release the butterfly from its shell, cut the thread that tethers the homing pigeon. May our Lord's will be done! Conformity to his dear will, that's what we want before anything, but next let us love him, let us desire him, let us possess him, let us see him.

Give me news, news of your novices, of dear Br Augustin ('the Kabyle who will not see it through'), remember me to him in our Lord and ask him to pray for me to his patron saint.

The refectory is now perfectly regular here, as are all the exercises, I could ask for nothing more, I live as at N.D. des Neiges, perfect regularity depends on no-one but myself. Pray with me that the community may be penetrated with a true spirit of poverty. Talk to me about God; make me a list, I beg you, of our duties as *Sponsi Christi* towards the divine spouse of our souls, I will use it in my meditations: what else have we to meditate on but our love and his?

God be with you; I would have liked to write at greater length but the intervals are short and I avoid asking for time as much as possible, or indeed for anything: 'ask for nothing unless it's a supreme necessity' is a maxim of St Theresa's which I try to put into practice, and every time I do so I am the better for it. God be with you, may he unite us in his love in this world and the next. Your humble, respectful and very affectionate son in our Lord,

Br Marie Albéric

JMJB N.D. du Sacré-Coeur,
16 June 1891 *(to Dom Martin)*

Reverend Father: It is now nearly a year since you accompanied me to Marseilles and I spent the final hours of my life in France with you, for I hope very much never to return there, I hope that God who consented to my coming here will let me stay here and live out my life in silence and oblivion. However I do not ask to be forgotten by the few people I dearly love, God forbid that I should fail to recognize so great a good. St Theresa said that her daughters, though detached from everything, were not detached from her, and nor am I from those to whom God has bound me. St Bernard would disown me a thousand times if I ever forgot my friends. Alas, I know only too well how to forget and am only too capable of doing so, but I don't want to, and I hope for God's grace to love more and more.

I often think of you, Reverend Father, and at this time especially I think of those last hours spent with you in Marseilles; I also think of your visit here next winter; by then it will be two years since you gave me the sacred habit, many links bind me to you. When, I wonder, shall we talk about all this in heaven?

There's little to tell you about myself, I go on in the same perfect health, the same deep peace, it pleases God to humour my weakness; in spite of that I'm very cowardly, attending to my body and seeking too much the consolations of the soul, with very little fidelity to grace; pray that I shall be less cowardly. However, I live according to the rule, at least I think so, and my external life seems to me exactly as it was at N.D. des Neiges. I am becoming more and more attached to Fr Prior, which will hardly surprise you, you must be used to seeing that the more people know him the more they love him. It depends on ourselves to be as regular as in any other Trappist monastery in France, the regular life functions very exactly and there is great fidelity to the customs and usages; you know all about this through Fr Prior, but it is such a consolation to me that I never tire of telling you about it.

I shall finish my letter because we are very busy at the moment, between hay and harvest, and the intervals are eaten up by holy poverty. Pray God that poverty always reigns as mistress in our convent and in our hearts; pray for me who have so much need of prayers, and for those I love and have left so as to serve our Lord with you. I kneel at your feet, Reverend Father, and ask you to bless me. Your very humble, respectful and devoted son in our Lord,

Br Marie Albéric

JMJB N.D. du Sacré-Coeur,
13 September 1891 *(to Dom Martin)*

Reverend Father: I wouldn't dare write to you on paper like this if I didn't know how much you cherish poverty, but you have told me your views on this subject so I shall offer no excuses. I have much to thank you for, Reverend Father, I always have much to thank you for when I write, but you don't like being thanked! Yet how can I not tell you how deeply touched I am by your visit to Madame de Bondy? I shall thank you before God because there you allow me to do so (I'm a poor wretch there, alas, as everywhere else), but I am so delighted that you have been to see her that I cannot not tell you direct, and surely you don't forbid me to tell you of my joys?

I hope you are well, Reverend Father, and that God spares you too many difficulties and leads you to him by a path not too beset with thorns; at all events I am sure he is leading you to him and that every step draws you closer to him, and this assurance is sweet to one who loves you, and your little disciple, your child, claims to love you in our Lord Jesus Christ.

Fr Prior told me this morning that perhaps another link will bind me to you. He plans that I shall make my profession on 2 February and he hopes that you may be here on that day: how happy I would be! If it is possible, do come, Reverend Father, you would make me so happy: you who gave me the sacred habit, come and continue your good work! I hope that God will wish it to happen like that.

I have little to tell you about my life: God keeps my body in health and my soul in peace, I follow from day to day the life of my brothers, always hoping that the next day will be better than the one before but, alas, always staying the same. I think I am more or less regular, the regular life is lived here, if I didn't follow it it would mean that I didn't want to follow it; but in fact the establishing of regularity in this dear little monastery is a joy for me, a joy for you. Every day I grow fonder of Fr Prior and Fr Polycarpe. What more is there to say? You see from all this that God is treating me like a child and giving me the peace and gentleness that my weakness needs. Despite all these benefits I am very cowardly! Pray, Reverend Father, for one who has great need of your prayers and also for those he loves. Pray for your very humble, devoted and respectful son in our Lord Jesus Christ,

Br Marie Albéric

JMJB N.D. du Sacré-Coeur,
Feast of St Martin, 11 November 1891 *(to Dom Martin)*

We have just come from matins, Reverend Father, and I want to wish you a happy feast before receiving holy communion for you with my brothers. No need to tell you how much I've been thinking of you since yesterday; every time the name Martin recurs in the glorious office of your great patron my thoughts fly to you and I ask God to make you more and more resemble him whose name you bear; a heavy responsibility lay on him too, he too had a flock to lead, may he protect you, he who now rests beside the good Shepherd!

If He so lovingly gathers to himself the least of his sheep who have nothing else to do than placidly follow the shepherd and graze on the green pastures where he leads them, what place will He not give the faithful shepherds who have defended their flocks from the cruel beast and taken on themselves their flocks' battles, trials and anxieties? You will be very close to God up there, you who have difficulties here below looking after his flock. But the course isn't finished down here yet, and you don't refuse hard work either; may St Martin help you, strengthen you, console you, and on the day when God thinks you have had enough, may your patron saint be at your side to drive away the cruel beast for the last time and lead you with him to the place where our Lord has wiped away all tears!

I hope God is consoling you, that you haven't too many worries, that you are in good health. Need I say how much I am looking forward to seeing you this winter? How I hope you will come early and stay long!

My profession draws nearer and nearer, less than three months now. What a grace that will be, to belong entirely to God! How unworthy I am and yet how I long for the day to arrive! I always need your prayers, but between now and my profession more than ever; I am sure you won't forget me and will commend me to all the fathers and brothers of N.D. des Neiges so that they will sustain me from afar and help me to become a good religious. I ask you of your charity also to commend to them Madame to Bondy, my departed grandfather, Abbé Huvelin to whom I owe so much, and Madame de Bondy's children.

There's little to say about myself, my life goes on just as you saw it at N.D. des Neiges; if there are changes within me I am not aware of them, which is to say that I am not progressing, always a lot of shortcomings, cowardice, pride, selfishness, not to mention all the rest! Certain vices should at least cure certain others! But no, they coexist in peace, and it is only charity, humility, renunciation, courage, in fact all the virtues, that are in abeyance. The body is in good health. From the point of view of regularity I am as I was at N.D. des Neiges. I see no difference; since 1 October we have been doing the winter exercises, we follow the customs and usages without a single alteration. The thing that pleases me very much, regarding the lack of a cloister and so on, is that I find it isn't an obstacle to regularity; God who has sent us here in these conditions gives us the necessary grace to be able to be regular without that aid.

God be with you, Reverend Father, and until very soon I hope. Believe the deep and respectful attachment in our Lord Jesus Christ of your humble and grateful servant and son,

Br Marie Albéric

N.D. du Sacré-Coeur,
12 December 1891 *(to Dom Martin)*

May Jesus
be always with you,
most Reverend Father!
Many thanks, Reverend Father, for the letter you wrote me on your return from Rome. You can guess why I haven't written to thank you for it earlier; until these last two or three days we were hoping that, as you were setting out at the beginning of this month, you would soon be among us. For me this was a great joy. But now, alas, your departure has been postponed and we shall not see you until the end of January. May God finally remove the obstacles and may you arrive on that date! I am awaiting your arrival with impatience and looking forward most eagerly to seeing you again, as surely you must sense - because it seems to me that these things can surely be sensed. I want to make up for not being able to wish you a happy new year by word of mouth (as I had hoped) by wishing it from afar, so I send you all my wishes, all my thoughts, and I pray God to answer them and bless ever more and more you and your intentions.

Please give my kind remembrances to dearest Fr Eugène, I pray God to make him a great saint too and to shower consolations upon him. And remember me to dear Br Norbert, tell him I never forget him and commend my cherished intentions and my poor self to his prayers. I think often and with great consolation of dear N.D. des Neiges where I received the sacred habit from you, where I spent the first months of my religious life amid so many graces, and where I found so much charity.

I'm afraid you're going to find me very cowardly, very slack, very unfaithful, very lukewarm; you will not withhold your remonstrances, will you, you will shake me up, rekindle me, put new life into me, of which, alas, I have great need. The fault is mine alone, for in addition to our dear Fr Prior I have a matchless novice master, a bright light and a wonderful example; what a grace for our little foundation to have such a shining light and such proven virtue!

God be with you, Reverend Father, and until very soon, I hope; please commend me very particularly to the prayers of the dear community of N.D. des Neiges and please give your blessing to your very humble, grateful and affectionate son in our Lord Jesus Christ,

Br Marie Albéric

JMJB N.D. du Sacré-Coeur,
by Alexandretta, Syria *(to Dom Martin)*
(No date, but certainly shortly after 2 February 1892)

Reverend Father: Heartfelt thanks for your blessing, for your letter, for the breviary and the copy of St Theresa which are doubly precious to me.

Although you were not present at my profession, which I very much regretted, I received your blessing by letter, which was very sweet for me, and I know you sent me a blessing from your heart on 2 February too. You are quite right to think that *our* breviary, given me to use on the day of my profession, will always be extremely dear to me, it's a token of remembrance that touches me deeply, thank you! And thank you for the St Theresa which hasn't yet arrived but will be so welcome on many grounds. I shall never be able to tell you how touched I am by your giving me these two precious books.

Now you must pray for me; pray that I may be a servant not of men, nor of myself, but of God alone, and of a humiliated and crucified God, as you say; pray the blessed Virgin that she may teach me to imitate and follow her son, to serve him and love him, and pray Saint Theresa that she may gain for me gratitude, fidelity, courage and the rest, and that she may teach me to pray to him to whom she prayed so well.

Pray for me a lot. God has let me pass my novitiate in inexpressible peace and consolation; he has fed my weakness on milk; he has given me infinite graces, conversion, religious vocation, vows, so many sweet and gentle things, so many benefits in my life! What do I owe him most? What special fidelity? Should not the person who receives more love more? I would love to love more, but alas! - so pray that I may love more; pray that I may love, that I may begin to love and serve my divine master humiliated and crucified. And pray too - I cannot leave you without asking it - pray too for those whom God has used so as to do me most good, and pray for Madame de Bondy and her family, pray too for my dear departed grandfather, pray for Abbé Huvelin.

I so look forward, as you know, to your visit; I hope it will be soon. My body is always in perfect health; God keeps my soul in deep peace: as for the rule, I think I'm just as I was at N.D. des Neiges, no more no less. You yourself will judge, you will put me right, that's what I need.

Fr Philomène has left us, I hope he is now with Him who inspired his wonderful charity and is praying for us in the happiness and the sight of our Lord.

I want to finish my letter as you did, your formula is so perfect: *Ad majorem Dei gloriam*; may this, by God's grace, be the rule of my life and the life of all our Lord's children. Give me your blessing, Reverend Father, and pray for your very humble, devoted and grateful son in our Lord Jesus Christ,

Br Marie Albéric

N.D. du Sacré-Coeur,
8 June 1892 *(to Fr Eugène)*

May JMJB be with you, dearest Father.
I begin like St Theresa; one can't, it seems to me, begin better, nor do better than by wishing this, nor express anything better in the whole letter. Pray God that I take from St Theresa not only external things but that I enter a little into her spirit, into the spirit of our Lord Jesus.

It's a long time since I wrote to you; my life has remained very much the same; God maintains my soul and body in peace and health, and this will go on as long as it pleases him. My life is one of work and prayer, inadequacy on both sides which will hardly surprise you; pray that this inadequacy may diminish and that zeal and courage may grow; for this more love is required, ask it for me. I read almost nothing: the holy gospels, the psalms, St Theresa in small gulps; it's true that the quality makes up for the quantity, the little I read is so good! Work plays a very important part here, which pleases me, not because I like work, but it is the companion of poverty, it's the imitation of our Lord, it's that which turns a Trappist monastery into a Nazareth.

I always praise God with my whole heart for having brought me here: not that everything is yet as it ought to be: to be alone with God in the universe is the first lesson Fr Polycarpe taught me and I bless him for it; thanks to it I proceed, if not without seeing, at least without stopping. If I really put this lesson into practice what sweet solitude I would have with God; even with my inadequacy I derive great benefit from it.

Try to send us some good novices, that's what we lack; but if God doesn't send them perhaps it's because we are not worthy. It is true, alas, that novices wouldn't find every desirable example of regularity here, but where would they find that? And they would certainly find good examples of humility, of charity, of courage in work. And you know, too, what a novice-master they would have in our dear Fr Polycarpe who sets such a perfect example and is such a bright light. As for Fr Prior, he is the most charitable, devoted and upright of men, as well you know. Pray for us. As for me, I am as I was at N.D. des Neiges, not much good, alas, neither humble nor charitable; I follow the rule which is no hardship to me thanks to the excellent health God gives me. Pray for Madame de Bondy, for her children who are growing up, for her husband, and pray for Abbé Huvelin and my grandfather.

God be with you, dearest Father, and may he give you the grace to give all your novices the good you gave me. I pray for you every day and I owe this to you. Your son in our Lord,

Br Marie Albéric

P.S. I am not writing to Dom Martin because I think he will be either here or on the sea when you get this; we have been awaiting notification of his arrival by every post since Easter.

Commend me to the prayers of my dear fathers and brothers. I think of them constantly with so much affection and gratitude, especially Fr Benoit, Fr Marie, Fr Apollinaire, and Brs Norbert, Alphonse, Xavier, Moise, Joachim, Sébastien, Toussaint.

N.D. du Sacré-Coeur,
by Alexandretta (Syria),
12 September 1892 *(to Dom Martin)*

JESUS

Reverend Father: It's a long time since I wrote to you which I regret all the more as I would have liked to thank you sooner for your excellent letter of 27 February. I was very touched by it and am so grateful for what you are asking God for me: to be a good religious, full of humility, poverty and obedience, yes, that is precisely what must be asked of God for me, to be a poor and humble workman with him, to lead the lowliest life with fidelity, love and gratitude, to be always in the last place, that dear last place which was so much his here below. Oh, always ask that for me, Reverend Father, that is how I understand life, there is where I seek it. But my sins make me unworthy of following our Lord so closely - pray a lot for me so as to make up for my own inadequacy.

This letter will find you in Rome whither you have been summoned to a very important meeting.[6] I must admit to having misgivings that a desire for improvement will involve changes distorting to our way of life. In our life of silence and solitude, in our life where every step is laid down by the holy rule, the governing body hasn't the same importance as it has in Orders dedicated to action. For us the important thing is our life within the monastery. To interfere in any way with this life - the life we are fortunate enough to have had handed down to us just as St Benedict planned it and just as it has been practised by our fathers St Robert, St Albéric, St Stephen and St Bernard - would be an action I could never forgive the abbots and capitular fathers of our congregation, for after all everyone, like you and me, made a vow on entering this holy order to follow its rule, they entered the order on purpose to follow it and were admitted as a result of a promise to follow it; they weren't admitted so as to destroy it, for to cease to follow it to the letter *is* to destroy it, and it was for the purpose of following it to the letter that the Cistercian order came into being.

That the order be divided into one or more observances is not important to us; it isn't the governmental organization of the order that drew us to become Trappists; we became Trappists so as to find the solitude, the poverty, the humble work, the penance which make our holy order unique in the Church, the only one where those whom our Lord has called to follow him in his hidden life in Nazareth can find their place. If anything were changed regarding this solitude, this poverty, this humble, lowly and blessed manual work, this penance, such as St Benedict prescribed them and St Bernard bequeathed them, I would be inconsolable, because the order would no longer be the one I entered with such joy.

Forgive all these words; these matters are important to me.

However, I want to speak of other things and to tell you before finishing this letter that I read St Theresa every day; may she draw me after her and enable me to follow behind her in the fragrance of her perfume. I also want to congratulate you on the foundation of N.D. de Bonrepos.[7] I am praying my best for this new daughter which, alas, is not saying much, and I pray for you, Reverend Father, and your intentions. I also want to tell you how I long for your visit. If I haven't written to you all this time it is because from Easter to July, and from one postal delivery to the next, we were expecting to see you. I am extremely anxious that you should come as soon as possible.

Pray for me, Reverend Father. I kneel at your feet to receive your blessing. Your very humble and loving son in our Lord Jesus Christ,

Br Marie Albéric

N.D. du Sacré-Coeur,
by Alexandretta (Syria),
12 September 1892 *(to Fr Eugène)*

JESUS be with you, dearest and most venerated Father.

Thank you, dearest Father, for your letter of 22 August. You mustn't think that I imagined myself forgotten for a moment because I haven't seen your dear handwriting for so long: I depend on you so much! Even if you never wrote to me I would still know that you were thinking about me with constancy and praying for me. However, do please write as often as you can, your letters are a joy and really do me good; by drawing nearer to each other we draw nearer to God; tell me your problems, your worries; the bond between us is greater when we share each other's burdens. God certainly isn't sparing you; after being overwhelmed with work at N.D. des Neiges you're now going to be sent to N.D. de Bonrepos, and as prior! God will help you. St Theresa without support and without a ducat is not much, but St Theresa with God is everything. The good Master will support you; he supported St Peter on the water; we are all walking on the water; what is life if not a dark sea? But the good Master is there; he lets you feel the power of the storm, the swell of the waves, because he knows you are faithful and belong to those he can test. As for me, I am not one of those, I am in my childhood, in my infancy, I have no fortitude, I am all cowardice, my faith is weak, so he keeps me in port. It is his hand that lets suffering and disquiet enter the soul, his hand that bestows peace. It is true, I am at peace, and I know that it is a pure gift, it has nothing to do with me; on the contrary, I have no grounds whatsoever for being pleased with myself, I do nothing well, I can only reproach myself on all sides, for the state of my soul, my lukewarmness, my huge vices, my cowardice; surely these ought to be a matter of grave concern to me, but I see it all, I see all this wretchedness, and yet remain in peace. Pray God that this does not betoken obduracy, sometimes I fear it does, yet I hope not, but how easily one can hope what one wants. Anyway, pray for me.

I think about my brothers as little as possible except to pray for them; I work alone, I spend my days either in church or cutting wood. I am in charge of the wood supply and I'm in charge alone. I love the work and I love the solitude, I'm not at all detached from my sisters the logs, but Fr Polycarpe tells me that there are no objections to this attachment. I read little, I read St Theresa with infinite delight. For reading and writing I come to the chapter-house and it's a marvellously edifying place; our good lay brothers come here often, never a word, never a sign, it's consoling to behold.

Good Fr Polycarpe has had a very bad summer, running a temperature continually, though these last two or three days he has seemed better - let's hope that the improvement persists now that the great heat is over. I cannot describe how good Fr Polycarpe and Fr Prior are to me. In fact all the monks and lay brothers are kind to me beyond words. I shall write to good Br Norbert as you tell me it would please him. I am happy to see in the list of your companions at N.D. de Bonrepos the good brothers Joachim and Sébastien. Commend me to the prayers of both of them as well as to those of Br Alphonse for whom I pray every day as was agreed. And remember me too to the other good fathers and brothers of N.D. des Neiges and N.D. de Bonrepos, to Fr Apollinaire, Fr Marie and Fr Géniez and to brothers Moise, Toussaint, François-Xavier and the others.

Go on praying for my cousin de Bondy, and for her dear ones, you know that this is the greatest charity you can do me. And I shall pray with my whole heart not only for you and your intentions but also for N.D. de Bonrepos, may you find our Lord there more and more every day until the hour comes when you find him totally. Pray for me and bless your son who is so respectfully and tenderly devoted to you,

Br Marie Albéric

N.D. du Sacré-Coeur,
by Alexandretta (Syria),
7 February 1893 *(to Fr Eugène)*

Thank you, dearest and most venerated Father, for your excellent letter of 7 December, thank you for your wishes for the new year, thank you for having thought of me on 2 February - that date seems to be becoming a blessed one for the religious of our little house, for again this year we had a profession, this time solemn. Good Fr Etienne is now completely Cistercian, may God continue to glorify himself in him as he has done up till now and more and more, for good Fr Etienne never ceases to set us the most perfect example in everything.

So you are now installed at N.D. de Bonrepos! May

our good Mother give you the sweet repose that you hope with such faith to find in her service; she has given it to you already and will, I'm sure, continue to do so - this repose is never refused to those who seek it only in God. Our repose - as I often tell myself, but never enough, my great cowardice requires that I repeat this truth over and over again for I am very cowardly, alas, far from being detached from myself - our repose is to rejoice in the infinite happiness of God and, looking somewhat lower, to rejoice in our crosses and always to seek for more, because it is through them that we have the happiness of imitating him and proving our love for him - things so precious to a heart that loves! Neither happiness nor God nor the cross will ever be lacking, in them lay our good Mother's sweet repose and in them lies the repose she offers to us. May we know how to savour it. You savour it I know, and I praise God that you do, but I am cowardly, I avoid renunciations and therefore do not repose as I should on her gentle breast, the most maternal that exists after her son's. However, wretched as I am, God keeps me in peace. He does so on purpose because of my weakness; knowing how incapable I am of facing the storm he keeps me becalmed. I see my faults but they don't disturb my peace. Pray God that this isn't obduracy!

Yes, I've been told that I'm going to do some theology, not without regret I admit, but there's no question of my taking Holy Orders and I hope I shall always remain more or less as I am. May God's will be done and not mine, but may God's will be done! That it shall be done I am convinced, for my superiors, like myself, seek nothing but it, and he will not refuse it to those who have no other concern than to do it as perfectly as possible.

I am sure you can guess how happy our dear and excellent Fr Martin's visit made me, and how much good it did. Do thank him, when you see him or write to him, and may people bless him for it - especially those who, like yourself, are dear to him - while waiting for our good Master to reward him.

God be with you, dearest and most venerated Father, the God who will repay you a hundredfold the good you have done me and always do me, and the good you do through your prayers to those I love. I commend myself as well as my cousin de Bondy, her husband and children to your prayers and those of your community. On my side I do not forget you in front of Him in whom I live. Your respectfully and tenderly devoted son,

Br Marie Albéric

N.D. du Sacré-Coeur,
by Alexandretta (Syria),
18 August 1893 *(to Fr Eugène)*

Thank you, dearest and most venerated Father, for your excellent letter which has just arrived by the last post; no need to tell you how sweet it is to hear your voice from far away, we know these things, we know that we love each other in our Lord. You are now at the head of your little monastery: I pity you, or rather I might be tempted to pity you, for can one in fact pity someone who is doing our Lord's will? Is there anything sweeter in the world than to do the will of the person we love? And if in doing it we encounter difficulties then the sweetness is doubled! Still, though I don't pity you, I sympathize with your problems; they couldn't not exist, and of every kind, both material and spiritual, the latter more painful, the former so opposed to our vocation that we would like to see them far away! But still, the problems of subsistence are certainly a part of poverty, and poverty is the imitation of our Lord, without it we cannot become saints nor follow him within this world in the perfect imitation that is so blessed; so from this point of view certain material difficulties have great value and are the richest of God's gifts.

I sometimes talk about you for I sometimes have permission to talk to our dear little Fr Louis de Gonzague;[8] he's just the same here as he was at N.D. des Neiges, a model, a daily inspiration, it's a joy to see him, to see such a pious soul, so simple, so brave, serving God with such matchless goodwill. The health of the body is little compared with the health of the soul, but I would like to give you news on that side too. He was very well up to the end of last month, but for the last three weeks he has been pulled down by two or three feverish attacks, I hope they're over now and that he won't have any more this year and that he will be able to resume community life (the attacks are not serious, everyone has them in these parts, I've been astonished he didn't succumb earlier).[9]

What shall I tell you about my soul? It's still more or less as you knew it, I still have a lot to do about humility, obedience, charity, meditation too, and many other things; it seems to me that where my soul is concerned I lose rather than gain; I ought to admit this as a tragic certainty; the only thing, basically, that prevents me from doing so, prevents me from admitting this sad fact, is my huge desire for it not to be true. May my inadequacy spur you to pray for me. I have no humility, no simplicity. What a huge sheet of paper I would need to enumerate all that I have too little of and all that I have too much of! And I'm terribly cowardly. As for my brother ass, it is marvellously well, it sets an example to the soul. I had a slight fever last autumn and was a little tired at the beginning of the winter, but since the end of Lent I've been stronger than ever.[10]

Pray God that I do his will, not mine, that I do what he wants of me, that I love him and serve him as he wants to be loved and served by me, that I console his heart as much as my wretchedness can! Pray too for Madame de Bondy, her children and her husband, don't forget them any more than me, I implore you; I owe them so much!

God be with you, dearest and most venerated Father. Bless from far away your very humble and very tenderly affectionate son in our Lord Jesus Christ,

Br Marie Albéric

III
In a new direction: letters from Rome (1896-1897)

This series of letters to Dom Martin de Gonzague and Fr Eugène having come to an abrupt end, the archives of N.D. des Neiges offer nothing more from Charles de Foucauld to his Trappist brothers until 1896. When Dom Louis de Gonzague ceased to be prior at Akbès in 1893 to become abbot of the important Trappist monastery at Staouéli, Algiers, Charles de Foucauld must certainly have written to him, but none of these letters have been preserved. On the suggestion of the Abbot General, Dom Sébastien Wyart, to whom he had written to ask to be dispensed from his vows, Charles de Foucauld himself went to Staouéli in September 1896 and thence moved on to Rome for reasons explained in the letters that follow: his life was taking on its new orientation. From Rome a voluminous correspondence started with Fr Jérôme (1878-1962) a novice whom he had met at Staouéli.

Rome,
Sunday 8 November 1896 *(To Fr Jérôme)*

May Jesus always be with you, dearest Father.
I am taking advantage of Sunday to write to you, dearest Father, but I certainly have not waited for the day of rest to pray for you.

The departure from Algiers was painful for all of us yet provided an opportunity to offer a sacrifice to God, which was a good, and a good that unites us more closely to our blessed Saviour is the greatest good and the only real good that exists - when we love, what is sweeter than to give something to the loved one, especially to give him something we hold dear, to suffer for love of him, to give him our very heart's blood. And then not only have we offered something to our Lord Jesus - our tears - but it is so marvellous that he lets us offer him these on behalf of each other, so that through our sacrifice we not only give *him* a sign of love but also do good to those we love.

I intended to describe our arrival in Rome, and here I am still at the departure from Algiers. You see, it was so painful for me. But God be praised and all pain be praised!

We arrived in Rome at 1.30 on Friday afternoon: we didn't leave the train at the San Paolo station near St Peter's because it wasn't really practicable, and how we praised God for it! Had we got out there we would have had to take cab after cab and it would have been really terrible for me to enter the city like that when St Peter and St Paul entered it so poorly, so wretchedly, and St Paul in chains. As it was we walked from the station to the Procura and on our way stopped at two churches where we knelt in adoration before the blessed Sacrament and asked that we might live here - in this city where we had just set foot - in conformity with his will, and we prayed him to bless all his children and especially those he has given us particularly to love: as you will guess, you were not forgotten in these two first visits to God: first we went to St Mary Major where our Lord's crib is preserved (and also, I think, St Jerome's remains) and then to the church of St Alphonsus where there is a picture of our Lady of perpetual succour, a title that suits the blessed Virgin so well! We need her perpetual succour so much, we who are weak and stumbling! For a long time now, and particularly for the last three years, I have been under her special protection. This is how it happened: three years ago I had many difficulties regarding my inner life - fears, anxieties, periods of darkness: I wanted to serve God, I was afraid of offending him, I couldn't see things straight, I suffered; so I placed myself with all my heart under the protection of our Lady of perpetual succour; I implored her to guide my footsteps as she had guided those of the infant Jesus, and to lead me in all things in such a way as not to offend God, but rather to be a subject of consolation for our Lord Jesus; in such a way as to console as much as I could the heart of Jesus that sees and loves us.[1] So it was very sweet for me to stand beneath the picture of our so dear and good Mother on my very first day, in my very first hour. Need I say that I commended you to her from all that is best in my heart, and I said for you as much as for myself, 'Our Lady of perpetual succour, grant me your all-powerful help and the grace always to ask for it'.

The day after our arrival, Saturday, we left the Procura early and went to St Peter's; it took one and a quarter hours. On our way we passed the Colosseum where so many martyrs have given their blood with joy and love for our Lord Jesus. How Jesus has been loved within those walls! What burning love has risen from there to heaven! How sweet it is to think that our Lord has been so loved! What are we beside those people? Yet we have hearts like them, our Lord loves us as much as them, and we can and must love him as much! How we must try to love this divine spouse of our souls! If our hearts are capable of loving passionately, and they are, let us drown in this love!

The Colosseum isn't far from where we are, I can see it from my window; it's there that St Ignatius was ground to pieces with joy for our Lord! There that this happened to thousands and thousands of martyrs! How those stones speak! What a song of love still rises from there to heaven! When we went to St Peter's we saw the windows of the Holy Father's apartments.

In St Peter's, after we had adored the blessed Sacrament and prayed at St Peter's tomb (I prayed that you would follow our Lord to your last breath as Peter did and console him to your utmost during your whole life), Fr Henri said holy mass a few paces from St Peter's remains, at an altar overlaying the bodies of the blessed apostles Simon and Jude; I served his mass and received God. Together we discharged our debt to Staouéli to St Peter himself. It was a great consolation to start our time in Rome in this way. Next day, Sunday, we continued our pilgrimage by going to the place of St Paul's martyrdom: it is marked by a pillar in a chapel a hundred yards from the monastery of the Three Fountains; from his place of martyrdom we went to where his body was taken after his execution and where it still remains. This is the church of St Paul. You can guess how large a part you played in this double pilgrimage in St Paul's honour, I commended you and myself as best I could to this apostle who loved Jesus so much, who worked so hard and suffered so much for him. May he draw us after him, you and me, and teach us how to love.

Fr Henri is well, rather exhausted by the journey and the complete change, but on the whole he's doing well and hasn't stopped. I hope you are well too, especially your soul, for what does the body matter? I cannot love you differently from how I love myself, nor desire for you anything other than what I desire for myself: to grow in virtue, to grow in the love of God, to do his will, to fulfil his desires, to love him passionately in thought, word and deed, to breathe nothing but his love and to console him as much as possible at every moment of our lives. I ask this for you with my whole heart, dearest Father, for I love you with my whole heart in the heart of our Lord Jesus,

Br Marie Albéric

Sunday 29 November 1896 *(to Fr Jérôme)*

May Jesus always be with you, dearest Father.
Thank you, dearest Father, for your two excellent letters. How right you are to talk to me at length about our Lord. It is certainly about him that we should talk, as two children talk of their father, or their brother, or their beloved, or whoever is their mutual all-in-all. And what are we if not two children? And how natural that we

should be united as we have only one thought, one intention, one desire, one love! Our two hearts are but one for we both want to breathe only for our Lord Jesus. And then, if two beings exist on earth who should speak only of God, surely they are you and me whose friendship has nothing earthly about it? We met briefly, we shall probably never meet again in this life, and yet we love each other, we love each other very tenderly in Jesus our saviour, we love as angels love each other in heaven insofar as this is possible for poor human beings. So, dearest brother, let our conversation be the conversation of angels, let us speak only of God under whose eye we both have our being; by talking together, by writing to each other, may the earth disappear and may we live already in the radiance of the other world, probably the only one where we shall meet again. But whereas angels have tongues of gold and hearts of fire, we stammer and are lukewarm; let us do what we can, and this is a reason for helping each other, for praying for each other, for loving each other all the more as we are weak and need to lean on each other from afar so as to follow our Lord Jesus along the painful way he has mapped out for us: 'Lift up your cross and follow me'.

I am enclosing a little flower I picked for you, while praying for you, in the catacomb of St Cecilia, beside her tomb, on her feast-day: may this martyr's flower remind you, as it does me (I picked one for myself too), of what the saints suffered and what we ought to wish to suffer ourselves. That's our advantage over the angels! If they were not in a state of bliss they would surely envy us our happiness at being able to suffer with and for our Lord Jesus! We have the best of it from this point of view! At least we have tears, we have sorrows perhaps, please God, and blood to offer our Lord in union with his tears, his sorrows and his blood! When I pray to my guardian angel I often ask him to make me do what he would do in my place. And how he would throw himself into suffering were he in my place! When I'm holding our cross and your medal in my hand I often pray to our guardian angels for both of us, that they may make us follow our Lord as they themselves would follow him were they on earth, and make us fulfil everything that our Beloved expects of us.

Thank you for the benefits you are bringing me by your prayers, and thank you for your affection and letters; God sees that I need help so he inspires you to do this; I praise him and thank you. Pray a lot: when we love we want to talk endlessly to the being we love, or at least look at him endlessly: this is what prayer is, familiar converse with our Beloved: we look at him, we tell him we love him, we rejoice at being at his feet, we tell him that this is where we want to live and die.

I hope you are making progress with your Latin; I want this very much for you: it's one of the best things to draw you close to our Lord: it will enable you to drink at the pure source of the early fathers of the Church, a source fragrant with the perfume of Jesus: those early fathers, St Athanasius, St John Chrysostom, St Augustine, St Jerome and the rest, are shining lights, burning flames, and I long to see you alight and aflame with their contact! Holy communion, reading and meditating on the holy gospels, prayer, reading the fathers, this is the nourishment I want for you, dearest Father, nourishment that the world does not know, but it carries us to the mountain of God like Elijah's bread, to eternal life like the Samaritan woman's water.

And, added to that, manual labour - inevitably relegated to second place at the moment because you, like me, are in your infancy: we are not yet old enough to work with St Joseph, we are still learning to read with the child Jesus at the blessed Virgin's knee, but manual labour, humble, lowly, despised, will have its place after a while, it's a large place, and then, with holy communion, the holy books, prayer, humble manual work, humiliation, suffering, and, to end up with, if it were pleasing to God, the death of a St Cecilia and so many others - if we have all this we shall lead the life of our Lord and beloved master Jesus.

And now I want to give you some advice, though I haven't the faintest authority to give you even a shred of it as I am neither a priest nor a scholar but only a sinner, indeed one thing alone authorizes me and that is my brotherly love for you in our Lord. My advice is to consult your spiritual director in everything, on everything, even the smallest matters; I say this because it has served me well to do that and served me ill to do otherwise, and I would like you to profit by my experience: the habit of asking what we should do even on the smallest matters has a thousand good results: it brings peace (for we are never in doubt); it forms a habit of self-conquest in everything (because in everything we renounce our own will); it encourages indifference to earthly things (because we are equally ready to do one thing as much as another); it causes us to perform a host of acts of love (to obey our confessor is to obey God, and to obey is to love, it is the act of love which is the purest, the most perfect, the highest, the most disinterested, the most *adorative*, if I may so put it); it fosters, especially at first, quite a few acts of mortification (after a while we see things in their proper perspective, we are detached from everything, we don't experience mortifications any more, or only rarely, but simply the joy of obeying); it causes all our actions without exception to be agreeable to our Lord Jesus and even the most agreeable that we can perform, so they are the most perfect actions possible (for, after all, our confessors do not always make us do the thing that is in itself most perfect, but the love, humility and goodwill that form the essence of our obedience would render our action done through obedience much more agreeable to God, much more perfect in itself; and when God sees this perfect obedience in his children, he always gives special illumination to confessors and causes them to know his special will regarding those who truly love, those who truly obey: St Theresa experienced this a hundred times and more).

After such a long sermon I can but beat my breast and ask your forgiveness for inflicting it on you. Forgive me, dear Father, dear brother, in consideration of my great fondness for you. St Theresa wrote that the more she loved someone the more she pestered them with interminable letters and sermons. I certainly have that in common with her. Thus the length of my letter has shown you how united I am with you in our Lord, you, my companion of eternity, for it is not in the temporal sphere that we are united, but by talking together we already have one foot in the life everlasting. Pray for your unworthy brother so that he may meet you there one day.

Your brother who loves you in the heart of Jesus,

Br Marie Albéric

Rome, 24 January 1897,
Feast of the Holy Family *(to Fr Jérôme)*

May Jesus be with you, dearest brother!
Thank you for your excellent letters, dearest Father. Thank you for talking to me about our Lord Jesus. How right you are! What would we speak of if not of him who is our life, for whom we breathe, for whom alone we want to live, to whom we belong unreservedly and for ever, body, soul, mind and heart, all to him, all for him! And how divinely good he is to allow ants like us to love him. One look from him would be too much for us: him, infinitude, sovereign and infinite perfection! us, such tiny, ungrateful, bad and sinning creatures. But not only does he look at us, he makes himself one of us; he 'takes delight in being with the children of men'; he watches over us and leads us in all our ways; he makes himself the least among us, suffers with us, for us and on behalf of us for thirty-three years, and dies through us and for us, bathing us and sanctifying all of us with his divine blood. How happy we are!

Thank you for confiding in me, for telling me about past griefs; if you haven't already thanked God for them, thank him now, offer them to him now - it's better to give thanks late than never: we give thanks for a benefit when we perceive that we have received one, and, as you say, all suffering is benefit. Fr de Ravignan says that while crying for our sins we must also thank God for them because he permitted them, permitted them as a benefit that will necessarily redound to his glory, either by sanctifying us through increased humility, penance, courage to repair the evil, gratitude towards a clement God, or by punishing us in a way that will demonstrate his infinite justice. Let us pray that we may never be among these last, but that we may always remain on the ladder of love that Jacob saw in a dream: the ladder the angels move up and down for all eternity, treading the rungs ceaselessly, for ever: admiration, contemplation, imitation, possession, union of heart and will, glorification of the Beloved, obedience. Obedience is the final, the highest, the most perfect of the rungs of love, the one where we ourselves cease to exist, where we are annihilated, where we die as Jesus died on the cross, where we hand over to the Beloved a body and soul without life, without will, with no movement of its own, a body and soul he can do what he likes with as with a corpse. There is absolutely no doubt that this is the highest rung of love, the rung that encompasses all the others, goes beyond them, is transcendant, above everything, beyond everything. It's the doctrine of all the saints, St Theresa's doctrine (labelled 'heavenly' in the bull of her canonization), Jesus's doctrine. So let us always obey with our whole soul and we shall always love with our whole soul. Let us give him this highest rung of love. Let us not give ourselves alive to our Lord, for he died for us. Let us give ourselves as he gave himself for us, dead, corpses, through perfect, unreserved, corpse-like obedience. Let us see how the angels obey; let us imitate them by saying with our whole heart: 'May your will be done in us as it is in heaven'. I, too, would like to open my heart, dearest brother in our Lord, and confide something to you that only my confessors and superiors know; so keep the secret until Rev Fr Abbot[2] tells you it is a secret no longer (even Fr Henri knows nothing about it). I have had to practise obedience a great deal this past week, and am having to do so still, and also courage. So I need your prayers: pray to the sacred Heart of Jesus, to our Lady of perpetual succour, to St Joseph, to the holy family whose feast is held in Rome on the third Sunday after Epiphany. Pray, too, to our guardian angels – of whom you gave me a medal.

For three-and-a-half years now I have been wanting to move from the rank of choir monk to that of serving monk, either in this Order or in some other religious Order in the east; I think this is my vocation: to go down. I made this request with my confessor's permission, but my superiors told me that before they could grant it I should go and spend some time at Staouéli. Imagine my surprise on arrival there to be told that I should proceed to Rome. Once here I assumed I would have a long wait before receiving the permission I longed for, I thought I would be here for two-and-a-half years, and then, without my asking anything, without my saying anything, our good and excellent Father General summons me to him, examines my state of mind, ponders my vocation, prays, assembles his advisers, and all unanimously declare that it is God's will that I should follow the path I so desire, of abjection, poverty and homely manual labour; the life of a Nazareth workman which He himself has for long been pointing to; so that now all the doors are wide open for me to cease to be a choir monk and descend to the rank of humble servant.

I received this news yesterday from the good and excellent Father General himself whose kindnesses to me touch me deeply. But it was before he had reached this decision that obedience was so necessary on my part. I had promised God I would do anything that Father General commanded me once the examination of my vocation had taken place, and anything that my confessor commanded. With the result that had they said, 'you're going to make your solemn vows in ten days' time', and later, 'you will receive Holy Orders', I would have obeyed with joy in the knowledge that I was doing God's will. Because by seeking nothing but God's will, and having superiors who were also seeking only that, it was impossible that God should not show us what it was. And now I am still in the hands of God and obedience.

I asked where I should go on leaving here in a few days' time: it will be to the east, but I have no idea to what house. God will tell me through the lips of my director. Shall I be able to go on writing to you, dearest brother? I have consulted Fr Louis de Gonzague about this and will do what he tells me; obedience again. You see how much I need my brother's prayers, but I'm dragging you down too, dearest brother - to be the brother of a servant, a humble labourer, is not brilliant in the world's eyes. But you are dead to the world and nothing can make you blush.

Thank you for opening your heart to me about your desire for the priesthood: I praise God with my whole soul for having awakened this desire in you, I do not doubt for a moment that it is your vocation and I thank God from the bottom of my heart: you've made me so happy with the news. There is no greater vocation in the world than the one to be a priest, and in fact it's no longer of the world, it's already of heaven. The priest is what we were saying just now about obedience - something transcendant, going beyond everything. He holds Jesus's divine body in his hands; by his voice he calls it into being on the altar; every day he brings Jesus to birth, like the eternal Father, like the most blessed Virgin; through baptism he brings souls to birth, through the sacrament of penance he purifies them, through communion he gives them our Lord's body as He himself did at the last supper, and at their death he helps them to appear before the Beloved by giving them their final adornment, their final perfume, their final forgiveness and their supreme strength. He converts souls by guiding them, by teaching them the gospel. Every single day of his life, whether in a convent or out in the world, he does what Jesus did during his three years of ministry - he teaches men to know, love and serve their good Master. What a vocation! He helps the divine shepherd to tend his flock, he helps him to carry the sick sheep on his back, he helps him to look for the sheep that is lost; he watches over the children of the Father's family and protects them against brigands; he procures the salvation of men's souls redeemed at such a price; he saves those for whom Jesus lived and suffered and died, those whom his sacred Heart loves with burning love, those for whose salvation he would suffer and be pierced again - it is the priest who saves them. Teaching the gospel, saving Jesus's children, giving them Christ's body from his hands! What a vocation, dear brother, and how I praise God for having given it to you. At one time I regretted not having received it myself, regretted not being invested with that holy character; it was at the height of the Armenian persecution - I would have liked to be a priest, to know the language of the poor persecuted Christians, to be able to go from village to village giving them the courage to die for their God. I was unworthy of it. But as for you, who knows what God has in store for you? The future is unknown. God leads us along such unexpected paths! Look how I've been led, tossed hither and thither for the last six months: Staouéli, Rome, and now the unknown. We are leaves in the wind, specks of dust, flakes of foam. Only let us be faithful, and with great love and obedience allow ourselves to be wafted where God's will is guiding us; in that way we shall give his heart the greatest possible consolation, until one last gust of blessed wind carries us to heaven. If ever obedience takes you to those distant shores where so many souls are lost through lack of priests, where the harvest is great but rots through lack of labourers, then give God abundant praise, for it is where we can do most good to others that it is best to be: complete self-forgetfulness, total devotion to our heavenly Father's children, that was our Lord's life, it's the life of every Christian, and especially the life of a priest. And if ever you are called to those countries where the people live in the shadow of death, be full of praise and devote yourself body and soul to bringing Christ's radiance to those souls sprinkled with his blood; you can do this as a Trappist with admirable results; obedience will show you the means.

I am glad to see you are reading Abbé Fouard and St Theresa: those two will teach you to know Jesus and to love all souls for his sake because he so loved them. May God take care of you and make of you a saint, dearest brother. I shall pray for you every day of my life. And don't forget your unworthy brother in your prayers. I pray the sacred Heart of Jesus that you may console it as much as possible in every moment of your life. Your brother who loves you in the sacred Heart of our Lord Jesus,

Br Marie Albéric

As a postscript to this important chapter a letter should be quoted from Dom Louis de Gonzague to his brother Dom Martin which states definitely that Charles de Foucauld, having been dispensed from his vows, is leaving the Trappists to follow his new orientation:

Staouéli, 11 February 1897. ...Fr Marie Albéric is definitely leaving the Order so as to go, I think, to Palestine and lead a hermit's life or something of the kind: for me it is a tragedy and a very great sorrow. I would have thought they wouldn't have rushed things through so cavalierly in Rome, but it must be admitted that his desires and wishes were very tenacious, to put it mildly. To tell the truth, though he sincerely loved various people in our Order - Fr Polycarpe, you, myself, and one or two others - he didn't really love the Order itself; he is a perfect specimen of our XIXth century nobility, brave, generous with its blood and its money, on occasions saintly, but incapable of sustained obedience and discipline under a leader; he could become a saint, I hope it for him, but in his own way, not through obedience. He has, I truly believe, made too many great and splendid sacrifices for God to allow him to stray, this is in my view his sole serious guarantee in the extraordinary life he is embarking on ...

IV
The hermit at Nazareth (1897-1900)

The archives at N.D. des Neiges do not hold many letters from Charles de Foucauld to his Trappist brothers during his hidden years with the Poor Clares at Nazareth - apart from the voluminous ones to Fr Jérôme. One or two to Dom Martin when tragic deaths caused the hermit to break his silence, one to the Abbot/Father General. The letters addressed to Dom Louis were unfortunately not preserved; that these existed, and in quantity, is known through Dom Louis' correspondence with Dom Martin.

Nazareth,
28 December 1897 *(to Fr Jérôme)*

May Jesus always be with you, dearest Father!
Thank you for your excellent letter of 27 November. I am absolutely delighted and praise God that you will not have to do military service, I really am so deeply happy about this. This is the first letter I have received from you since being in Nazareth, the one of early November which you say crossed mine is therefore lost, which is not surprising with the Turkish post. You'll have to tell me again what you told me about yourself in that letter, dear Father and brother in Jesus, it interests me deeply. I'm delighted, too, that you're spending another year at Staouéli. I would like you to spend several more years in that dear house if the means can be found, near to your good abbot and director, in the cradle of your religious life, with that good community and protected by that

admirable enclosure; a good enclosure that imprisons us with our divine spouse is such a benefit! What sweet captivity! I am very solitary here, much more solitary, much more silent than when I was a Trappist; God is spoiling me, but you have the advantage over me of being as if in a well with Jesus.

Tell me about your studies. Where are you up to? When are you going to start philosophy? You must study well, not for yourself but for Jesus, because he commands it through your superior, because he commands it through the voice of his Church, because it is the Church's will that priests should be men of learning. How can they lead others if they themselves are blind? 'Both will fall into the ditch'. Moreover religious education is useful for loving God. We can only love what we know, and we love more and better as we know more perfectly! Sound theological teaching will make you know God and love him, will make you know his will and do it, will make you glorify him through your actions. To acquire sound theology it is indispensable to have a sound knowledge of philosophy, and for both it is indispensable to have a firm grasp of Latin. You see how everything hangs together! Study and pray, not for yourself, but everything for Jesus! Pray so as to love him, serve him, obey him and glorify him, and cause him to be glorified by his other children.[1] Study so as to love him, serve him, obey him and glorify him, and cause him to be glorified by his other children! Everything for him alone. Everything with a view to him alone. All your thoughts, words and actions tending to this one end, ordered to this one end. To glorify God as much as you possibly can by perfecting yourself as much as you possibly can and by perfecting your neighbour as much as you possibly can, and all solely with a view to him.

That is your life, your daily life, until death, until the time comes when you will glorify him eternally in heaven. Oh Father and beloved brother, pray for me, pray for me who am a miserable sinner and do so little of all the things I hold up to you, who sanctify myself and others so little, who glorify Jesus neither in myself nor in others, who am so wretched and unworthy!

But as for you, I would like you to be perfect, I would like you to do the good that I fail to do. God is giving you *the* most holy vocation, the vocation to the priesthood. May he be praised! But with what love, what zeal, must you prepare yourself for this grace. Pray and work. By work I mean study, in the measure that obedience will dictate: 'He who loves me keeps my commandments', 'He who hears you, hears me'. The voice of Fr Louis de Gonzague is for you the voice of Jesus, and I know he is guiding you along this twofold path: prayer - communion, silent prayer, the rosary, the way of the cross, well-chosen holy reading; and study - study with a view to loving and serving. Everything for Jesus.

Thank you for your prayers, beloved brother, thank you for remembering those that I must love more particularly; but it's all men, isn't it, that we hold in our hearts as they are in the heart of Jesus. Yet his heart wants us to love some more than others as he wants you and me to love each other. I shall pray faithfully for your parents. Thank you for telling me that sad thing, my brother in Jesus! May our Lord give you a good Christmas and a holy year. May you do his will this year and always! Amen.

I am sending you a picture that was given me by a saint, someone who has founded five convents of Poor Clares, someone very fervent and austere on whom God showers graces and crosses. And the flowers I'm sending come from a place whence you can see Gethsemane, the Mount of Olives and Bethlehem. Suffering, contemplation, self-forgetfulness, losing ourselves in the joy of the glory and bliss of Jesus.

Your brother who loves you in the heart of our Lord Jesus,

Br Marie Albéric

(Nazareth),
15 February (1898) *(to Fr Jérôme)*

Thank you, dearest Father, dearest brother in Jesus, for your letter on St Albéric's day. Yes, those are the sentiments I like to see in you, yes, it's indifference to everything except Jesus and his will; doing this or doing that, what does it matter? but doing the will of Jesus, yes, that always, with all our strength and all our being. You did very well not to ask when you would start philosophy, because what does it matter to you? Jesus has given you, child as you are, a teacher, our good Reverend Father, and has told you 'he who hears him, hears me'; the more you listen blindly to him the more you listen blindly to Jesus and the more you show your love for Jesus. Go on, go on in holy indifference, indifference to everything but Jesus's will, and his will is conveyed to you by your superior and your director; they are for you a single and very worthy and very beloved person, as for St Theresa in the last years of her life. But while asking nothing and desiring nothing, you must take care not to suppress any detail of what is happening in your soul: if a desire, a fear, a temptation, a good thought springs up in you, emerges in you, don't conceal it through humility or self-mortification or a desire to remain in a state of indifference, but tell him everything, adding that you ask for nothing, desire nothing but Jesus, and that you are giving an account of your soul, taking stock of it: this is indispensable if a director is to guide, for he guides a soul not by following his own ideas but by following what he sees to be God's designs on it, and he recognizes these designs by and large by seeing what God has put into the soul, the aspirations he has sent it, the ordeals he has subjected it to. The director guides a soul not according to himself but according to God, and this is made difficult for him if the soul withholds complete and unrestrained openness and so prevents him from getting a clear picture of the way God is guiding it. Thus absolute indifference except to Jesus, his glory, his consolation, his will: but absolute openness, the simplicity of a child, telling everything to your beloved director, the good, the bad, the indifferent. I thank God on your behalf, dearest brother, for giving you such a good director and one whom it is so easy for you not only to obey but to love with tender and filial devotion. This is a great grace that the ever-merciful Jesus has granted you.

That is why I asked you when you were starting your philosophy! Because before you start I would have liked you to prepare the way by a sort of retreat of just a few days, not an ordinary retreat, but a reading retreat, during which, without appreciably increasing your meditation time or making yourself conspicuous, you could use the time normally devoted to work and study to reading five small volumes (a matter of ten days at the most) containing the encyclicals, letters and so on of Leo XIII: nothing would be better in my view, before starting your Christian and religious studies, than to have the way paved by his great and lofty soul, a soul imbued with the grace to show us the way and the truth and to give us the life of the soul in the name of Jesus. The five small volumes cost five francs in all and are published in Paris by the Assumptionists of rue François 1er. If, when the time comes, Reverend Father approves this idea, so much the better; if he turns it down, again so much the better. It's always so much the better for children of obedience. 'He who hears you, hears me'; all we have to do is to listen to Jesus, what does anything else matter to us?

So much the better, too, if you do Greek. 'He who hears you, hears me', always so much the better, and in any case I am pleased that you should be doing Greek; it is absolutely indispensable for a good grasp of theology, and this you must have, it's essential for serving God really well in the priesthood (how can a man who hasn't got the light give it to others?). My Greek, alas, is almost forgotten, but the little I still have has been invaluable. Moreover it's a study very sweet to the heart because it's the language of the New Testament; everyone spoke it in Judaea at the time of Our Lord. He must have spoken it more than once himself though in the normal way he spoke the language of the people, Aramaic; this consideration alone makes Greek sweet and sacred to our hearts. But the sweetest thing is Jesus's voice saying, 'He who hears you, hears me', and thereby giving you, through obedience, the most precious thing to a heart that loves, the means of knowing and doing the Beloved's will.

I am sending you today by registered mail, addressed to Reverend Father, my meditations on the holy gospels. When I left Rome I lost my taste for writing. But I found myself in periods of such aridity and so incapable of praying that I asked my spiritual director whether I should continue not writing or take up my written meditations again. He answered, 'Write down your meditations, it's a very good method of meditating, and particularly useful for you because it will help you to organize your thoughts'. So I write every evening. You'll find these meditations different from the others: these are often more like prayers, homely conversations with the divine spouse of our souls, I tell him everything I have to tell him, it's very intimate, but I don't want to have secrets from you, dear brother in Jesus. In heaven you will see into the depths of my soul, so why not start now? One thing I ask - that you keep these notebooks, so that if I ever need them in the future I can ask you for them; I don't suppose the occasion will arise but I would like to take this precaution; I have often destroyed meditations of this kind in the past and then regretted it, realizing that they would have been useful to me. I tell you this so that you can profit by my experience. Keep all and every note you make; later on, when you least expect it, such and such a series of notes will turn out to be useful. Keep everything in an orderly way and don't destroy: that's what I do now.

Indifference, too, about remaining at Staouéli or going to wherever God wants. I would certainly like to see you never leaving Staouéli, but you must follow God first and foremost: if he leaves you there, so much the better a thousand times; if he takes you to the Lebanon for a while, we shall still praise him; he can bring good out of everything; it is for us to be faithful, and the prime means is by conformity to his will. 'He who hears you, hears me'. Wherever your director sends you, there is the place for you to be, there is where Jesus wants you, there you will find the graces he has prepared for you, there you will see the blossoming of the flowers he wants to bring to life in you, there you will find all you want in this world because there you will find the fulfilment of his beloved will. But I must add one thing, which is that I'm absolutely overjoyed to hear that it's been definitely decided that you're not to do military service - an activity so little in accord with Jesus's disciples. And another thing: if you find you cannot stay at Staouéli I would be overjoyed to see you with the Capuchins, the flower of the Franciscan order, fervent, poor, austere, men of prayer. And I would also be glad to see you in the Lebanon, biblical country, mentioned in every line of the Song of Songs.

And it fills me with joy, beloved brother in Jesus, huge, deep joy, to hear that you are going to be more closely united with our Lord through receiving minor orders. Everything that binds you to the Church, the bride, binds you to Jesus, the bridegroom. So each new order that you receive will be a joy to me: it'll form yet another bond between you and the Saviour, and how priceless to the loving heart are the chains that bind it to the Beloved! How I shall bless those chains that step by step bind you more narrowly to him! Oh I shall be so close to you on that day beseeching Jesus to tighten, always to tighten the links that bind you to him, beseeching him to clasp you to his heart and always hold you there, in this life and the next.

I see it as a special mark of our Lord's kindness that he has chosen the Annunciation to be the feast on which you will receive your orders, a feast of the blessed Virgin, our Mother, the one when she said the words that should always be our words too: '*Ecce ancilla Domini; fiat mihi secundum verbum tuum*'. In the past Cistercians were ordained not only in the name of holy poverty but also in the name of the blessed virgin Mary, to show that we are entirely her sons. But if the whole Order belongs to her, I would like *you* to belong to her in a very special way. It is customary on feast-days to offer wishes. This 25 March will be a great feast for me because it will be a great feast for my brother, and I shall wish you two things: first, to be a faithful child of Mary throughout your whole life, remembering that to be true brothers of Jesus we must be true sons of Mary; and second, to have the words uttered by our Mother on that day always in your heart, on your lips, in your actions: '*Ecce ancilla Domini; fiat mihi secundum verbum tuum*'; to live every moment of your life as a faithful servant of Jesus, and therefore to act every moment of your life according to his word, according to his will, always, always to do his will like a good servant, like our Mother, in this life and the next, everlastingly, as from today.

And you already know how to do his will: 'He who hears you, hears me'; it is through obedience. This is absolutely proven and wonderfully perfect, for every act of obedience to those to whom we are lawfully subject in the sight of God is not obedience to a man but obedience to God through pure love of him; the act of obedience to a man, or which seems such, is thus really an act of pure love for God. In addition to obedience, to the fulfilling of God's will which is the hall-mark of the good servant, the '*ancilla Domini*', in addition to filial love, the state of sonship, the sense well-grounded in your soul that you are Mary's son and Jesus's brother, I would advise - in order to keep your love for your Mother in good shape - a means that I myself use, namely to prepare very well for her feast-days, to celebrate them well, with great gladness, to wish her a happy feast with Jesus, in all simplicity, like her child, to offer her something, be happy, rejoice in her being so beautiful in God's eyes. Do what I do on the blessed Virgin's feast-days; I always find a sermon by some father of the Church, in French or Latin, about the feast-day in question, or another one, so long as it's about the blessed Virgin, and I go to church and read it there, as near to the blessed

Sacrament as possible, and I read either a few pages or one or two lines, because when God impels me to move on from reading to prayer I follow this movement. If prayer flags then I return to the book; if it doesn't come at all then I keep to the book; if it comes and the blessed Virgin maintains me in a state of sweet prayer at her feet, I put the book aside and leave it there. I recommend this way of celebrating our Mother, letting ourselves be led to her by one of the great doctors of the Church, and going to find her close to her son in the blessed Sacrament.

The Annunciation is the feast of Nazareth; the cave that formed part of the holy family's house and was its most hidden spot, and where the annunciation took place, is still there; soon I shall go there and deposit the wretchedly inadequate picture I am sending you - of my own composition; every morning from 17 to 25 March, throughout that whole novena, I shall hear mass, receive holy communion and say a rosary for you in the very cave of the annunciation, asking God to grant you through the most blessed Virgin the two things I wish for you, the things that contain everything else; for to do God's will is to glorify him as much as possible, and that is everything. May Mary be your mother in this life and for ever in the next, may Jesus be your brother and your spouse, may you serve him perfectly, glorify him perfectly, console his heart with all your might in every moment of your life - that's what your brother asks for you, your brother who loves you in the sacred heart of Jesus,

Br Marie Albéric

There are three things to note about the following letter: that Fr Jérôme has been sent to Rome for a period; that Charles de Foucauld now signs himself Br Charles (instead of Br Marie Albéric); and that at the top of the letter there is a device that heads nearly all his letters henceforward - a heart topped by a cross followed by IESUS CARITAS (or sometimes IESUS/FIAT VOLUNTAS TUA).

Jerusalem,
2 January 1899 *(to Fr Jérôme)*

Beloved brother in Jesus: Thank you for your excellent letter of 5 December. It has found me in Jerusalem. The Poor Clares of Nazareth and those of Jerusalem are so united that they share everything, including Br Charles. They asked me if I would go to their convent in Jerusalem where I would be of more use; I remembered that 'when you are asked to go a thousand paces, you must go two thousand', I consulted my spiritual director, he said yes, so I came. As always when one leaves a good thing for God's sake and by his command, I have found even better things than I had before. When God asks us to make a sacrifice it's always so as to give us a grace. The abbess (pray for her; you must if you love me) has organized a hermit's life for me. She gives me the work I need to earn my bread, but I do it in my cell as and when it suits me. The convent is two kilometres from the town on the road to Bethlehem. I have a little boarded cell in a small enclosure right next to the cloister - from my window I see my much-loved Bethany and, beyond, the dark curtain of the mountains of the Jordan. I never go out except to the chapel, so I have been able to organize a hermit's life for myself and I deeply enjoy this marvellous solitude. No-one knows me except the abbess.

And it is surely the same for you, beloved brother: the sacrifice that God has asked of you by moving you from Staouéli will be a source of many graces for you. What these graces will be I do not know, but you must surely be receiving them. I already discern various visible ones (without counting those which only He knows about): for instance, the sacrifice of the departure from Staouéli offered to God; those areas of darkness which are a sign that God wants to lead your soul forward; the grace he is granting you by putting you in Rome under the guidance of Fr General and Fr Robert who are abler spiritual directors than any of the directors you had at Staouéli, however loved and holy they may have been; the very air one breathes in that cherished and blessed Rome - all these are favours, excellent favours, incomparable acts of mercy towards you on God's part, and I in my blindness can see only an infinitesimal part of his blessings. Moreover, dearest brother, your letter brought me great joy on three particular scores: first, because it revealed the perfect purity of your intention to live for God alone; second, because it showed the darkness and inner suffering that God has plunged you into, a sure sign that he wants you to make great strides in his love; and third, because you said you were under the direction of Fr General and Fr Robert.

Yes, beloved brother, I have decided with all my heart that the graces I shall ask for at holy communion during these first nine days of January shall all be for you. But I shall not ask for light, because darkness is perhaps more salutary for you at the moment: we must let the divine shepherd feed us on the pasture of his choosing and, whether sweet or bitter, we must accept it from his hand; if he thinks you need darkness then it is there that I, too, want you to remain, in pain and suffering, for as long as it is good for your soul. I shall ask him during these nine days, and every day, that you shall glorify him to the utmost and to this end that you shall love him to the utmost. It is for him to choose the means. We ourselves are blind, and when we lack God's grace to guide a soul in his name we are like those children mentioned in Jonas who can't tell the right hand from the left. Let us ask for nothing but to glorify our Beloved and to that end to love him to the utmost. There is much to be said about the advantages of interior darkness, indeed the absolute necessity of it, if we are to advance in the love of God. St John of the Cross wrote three divine volumes on the subject. Steep yourself in this truth; that ever since Adam's sin no-one can prosper in the material or spiritual order except through hard labour proportionate to the good achieved, and as spiritual goods are of an infinitely higher order, and as the love of God is the good of goods, these can only be bought at the price of hard labour that reaches the point of suffering, suffering that is ever keener as the good towards which we are tending is higher. The interior darkness and suffering encountered by the soul in its inner life of divine love is the only thing sufficiently crucifying to serve as the price, as the money if I may so put it, for the purchase of divine love, our supreme good; which is why we cannot achieve loving God except by purchasing our love through interior darkness and suffering proportionate to the love we shall ultimately reach. So, far from being anxious or worried about your periods of darkness and trying desperately to get out of them, you should thank God who, in ineffable goodness, is using them to bring you the absolutely necessary means of growing by great strides in his holy love and thus continuing the series of priceless blessings that he has bestowed on your soul.

But when you are in this state, if you want to cooperate with grace and respond to the favour of these periods of darkness, you must as always and more than ever do what you have to do: (1) you must have intention; you must have the firm and pure will to live for God alone, to seek in everything not your own good or the good of some other creature but the good of God alone; 'to love', as St Thomas put it, 'is to desire the good of the loved one'. This purity of will is your first duty. Number 2 is obedience: 'He who hears you, hears me'. Ever since Jesus said those words our periods of darkness can never be a threat, for by means of those words we can resemble him perfectly at every moment of our lives, do at every moment what he did at every moment, be perfect. The divine will which he ceaselessly saw in himself and to which he never ceased to conform his own (herein lay his perfection) - we, too, can experience, because on all matters we can consult those of whom the Truth said: 'He who hears you, hears me'. For you this means your superiors and your director, Fr General, Fr Abbot of Staouéli and Fr Robert. And in this I so intensely admire God's goodness towards you. He has arranged things, organized events, inspired spirits in such a way as to give you, in Rome, without prejudice to our excellent and well-loved Fr Louis de Gonzague, and in the person of our Fr General and our dear Fr Robert, two outstandingly good spiritual masters, two outstanding guides to the inner life. I personally set such store by their guidance that not only do I ceaselessly praise God for having had it myself when in Rome, but I also made up my mind long ago and after much thought that I would go to Fr Robert were God to take Abbé Huvelin from me, my spiritual director who fathered my coming to Jesus twelve years ago. Not to Fr General because he is too busy to take on the exacting work of individual spiritual direction, and because he is so at one with Fr Robert that their two guidances are not two but one. I am talking to you from my innermost heart, dear brother, I have never told this to anyone else. The truth is that among all the Trappist monks I have known, Fr General and Fr Robert are the two souls in whom I have much the most confidence as spiritual directors; I find them so superior to anything else I have known, with the exception of Abbé Huvelin, that were God to take this beloved father from me I would immediately have recourse to those two whom I regard as one: they are so high in God, both of them, that there would always be agreement in the guidance they give a soul. When I was in Rome I laid my soul bare to them completely and utterly, and I obeyed them without stint, while still remaining in the obedience and filial love due to our dear Fr Louis de Gonzague. And how marvellously God has led me - by means of the blessed obedience I gave to those two holy interpreters of his will! 'He who hears you, hears me'. In listening to them I gave him the means of leading me where he wanted me to go.

You probably remember that at Staouéli I thought I could not do you a greater service than to advise you to take our beloved Fr Louis as confessor and director. Now, dearest brother, I think I cannot do you a greater service than to advise you to do what I did and would do again, take Fr Robert as confessor and director, and at the same time profit by the grace God has given you - of being very near Fr General - to receive his guidance too.

Open your soul to both of them without stint, so that they may know you to the depths, so that they may see your inner life stripped naked, do not have the ghost of a secret from them; and then consult Fr Robert in everything, great and small, talk to him often, get really close to him, tell him all about your inner life, let him take a lamp into all the recesses, all the secret places of your soul, while you praise God for having prepared so bright and gentle a light for you. In addition go sometimes to Fr General - if he thinks fit he will fix the days and times of your visits - and profit by his teaching on your inner life; I vividly remember the final directives he gave me and have often praised God for giving them to me through his lips, they have frequently sustained me, consoled me, enlightened me. You must do the same. Absolute unbounded openness with Fr General and Fr Robert; continuous guidance at every moment from Fr Robert, and guidance insofar as he judges it useful from Fr General: this is what I ask you to do; it's what I myself did; and all of it without in any way detracting from the filial love and religious obedience which you owe our beloved Fr Louis de Gonzague; this is what I did. I see it as a very special favour from God to have placed you when still so young under the spiritual guidance of two such supreme masters of the inner life as Fr General and Fr Robert: let me repeat that with the exception of Abbé Huvelin I have never found their equal in this field, or anything approaching it, and if I were deprived of Abbé Huvelin I would immediately have recourse to them. I need hardly say that it is not enough to consult them and open yourself to them, you must also obey them with the love, faith and joy that you experience in obeying Jesus who said: 'He who hears you, hears me'. When Fr General decided that I should leave the Trappists, I was equally ready to leave or stay, I didn't pray God to let me leave or let me stay, my constant prayer was that he would do with me whatever would best glorify him; I assure you that I expected Fr General to decide that I should stay rather than leave: God blessed this way of doing things and my total obedience allowed him to lead me where he wished. I always practised total obedience in my religious life and I still do (for I am wholly, but wholly, under obedience to Abbé Huvelin) and I marvel at the results of this blessed obedience: everything that was done to keep me with the Trappists - either by others or myself - was turned by God through my obedience in such a way as to enable me to leave. Therefore obey, obey with complete openness of soul, obey the love you have for Jesus, the faith you have in his divine word, the joy of doing with certainty the Beloved's will, of doing what he himself would do in your place, the most perfect thing to do because it is in conformity with the divine will ('He who hears you, hears me') - the will to which Jesus was united at every moment of his life, in which alone perfection lies, outside which there is no perfection, no imitation of Jesus, no harmony with Jesus, no love for Jesus, for anyone who does not do God's will at any given moment immediately ceases to imitate Jesus, ceases to be perfect, ceases to be in harmony with Jesus, ceases to love him; and we know God's will at every moment through obedience: 'He who hears you, hears me'.

Thus obey Fr General and Fr Robert until the time comes when God will give you back our dearest Fr Abbot of Staouéli for whom you will have kept a warm affection and the filial love and obedience that he deserves on so many counts.

Openness and perfect obedience to Fr General and Fr Robert, this is the sole burden of my letter. Forgive me my bad example in writing at such length. It would be good for you to read a little of St John of the Cross; I shall copy out some passages and send them to you.

You offer me your brotherly services from dear Rome. I accept your offer and ask you (having obtained the necessary authorization) to be so good as to send me by registered mail the ordo for the breviary and the mass as used by the Roman clergy. I still recite the breviary and in my great love for Rome would like to say it as the Roman priests do, as I myself am bound to nothing. But

I haven't got the ordo for 1899. Two other commissions: if ever you're in front of the picture of our Lady of perpetual succour, or the pillar marking the place of St Paul's martyrdom, spare a thought for me in the presence of our communal Mother and of him who so urgently 'preached the charity of Christ'. Thank you a thousand times in advance.

Oh no, as you can see by this letter, I am very far from forgetting Fr Robert, or the good and dear Fr de Gonzague de St Isidore, or any of the people in that dear mother-house; I pray for it every day! And every day for you, beloved brother, whom I love with all my heart in the sacred Heart of our beloved Lord Jesus.

Br Charles

Nazareth,
8 May 1899 *(to Fr Jérôme)*

Dearest Father: Thank you for your excellent letter of 5 April and the precious enclosures: the leaf from the orange-tree and the marvellous reproduction of the holy shroud: that photograph is a treasure, a true portrait of our Beloved, I cannot thank you enough; it is a true relic and very precious, thank you a thousand times!

I was determined to write to you before 1 June, dear brother in Jesus, to tell you how close I shall be to you on the feast of the sacred Heart, thinking both of your simple vows three years ago and your solemn profession whose date I don't know but it must be soon. Three years ago you became the spouse of Jesus; at every moment of your life pursue what this name calls you to do; at every moment of your life be what a spouse of Jesus ought to be - this embraces everything.

I'm sending you a sister, a mirror, a protectress, a consoler, in the shape of Sister Beatrix, a carmelite nun who died in a Spanish convent 300 years ago. I discovered her in some pages written by St Theresa - I'm sending you the three pages in question; read them when you're sad, arid, bad, sorely tried within and without;

learn from them to be always calm and to accept 'every trial as a tender token of love from the hand of your brother Jesus'. And read them sometimes when you're examining your conscience and see if you resemble our dear Sister Beatrix; her gentle radiant countenance is a real 'vision of peace'; pray to her, she will protect you. I pray to her oh so often!

At this moment I'm reading a jewel of a little book - Fr Caussade's *Traité de l'abandon* abridged and introduced by Fr Ramière. If you every come across it read it and read it again; I've been reading and re-reading it for two-and-a-half years and I always find new things in it. I think it would be very useful for you too, very profitable. But, when you read it, mind you read Fr Ramière's introduction first because this is necessary for a proper understanding.

Please thank Fr General a thousand times: I am deeply touched and grateful for his message, his kindness, his ever-open arms. I continue to love him with filial love, to see myself as his child, to love the Trappists and to pray for him and the whole Order. I am as ever under full and total obedience to Abbé Huvelin, 'like a corpse'.

The more I am in this part of the world the more I love the Trappists. The other Orders seem incapable of producing any real good in barbarous countries, whereas the Order of St Benedict and St Bernard is admirably suited to accomplishing today in the east what it accomplished in the past in Europe. It is *the* apostolic Order *par excellence.* I long so much to see the Trappists growing and developing in these lands!

Please also thank dearest Fr Robert for his message and his prayers. Tell him he has his place in mine, and also in my heart, and that I remain his devoted and faithful child.

Let us detach ourselves, dearest brother, let us empty our hearts of all created things so that they may be filled with Jesus. Let us detach ourselves! Let us receive as an outstanding grace everything that detaches us!

Next time you write, instead of putting Brother

Charles Foucauld on the envelope, put Brother Charles of Jesus. Abbé Huvelin has given me permission to adopt this simple name in future; pray that it may be the sign of the thing! Let us both belong to Jesus, like faithful brides of the one and only Bridegroom!

Your brother who loves you in the sacred Heart of our Lord Jesus,

Br Charles of Jesus

27 October 1899 *(to Fr Jérôme)*

Beloved Father and brother in Jesus: Since my last letter our Lord has let you feel his cross. *Bona crux*! - isn't that always so? And let us be men of faith, of that faith by which 'the just live', men of faith, hope and love. 'All the hairs of our head are counted. Not a sparrow falls to the ground without the will of our Father. Seek the kingdom of God and all the rest will be added to you'. Yes, don't be afraid, however things may seem; what the present moment brings is infinitely good for our soul, it is God's will, 'everything that happens is for the good of those who love him'. Rome, Staouéli, France, the east, places, accidents, difficulties, obstacles – all will show us at every moment a more perfect thing to be done: let us do it at every moment and 'all the rest will be added to us' Faith, hope, love. And then, dearest brother, the time has come for us to stop living on earth, the darker the day the more must we leave it to live only in heaven. Let us accomplish here below the duty that the moment brings, perfectly and at every moment, but apart from that let our hearts and minds be in heaven, high up above the sad mists of the earth, always in the radiant atmosphere of faith, hope and love, thinking only of Jesus, remembering only Jesus, loving only Jesus, him alone, the spouse, filling our mind, our memory and our heart. '*Sursum corda*'. May our conversation be in heaven. '*Quae sursum sunt quaerite, non quae super terram*!' Let us forget this poor world, as Mary and Joseph did at Jesus's feet. Let us live here as if not living here, let us walk here as if in a dream, and let our real life, our spirit, be always lost in heaven.

Wherever this letter finds you, dearest brother, and in whatever state or condition, be assured that I am praying for you with my whole heart and that I long to know the final decision. I have always longed and still long for you to escape military service at any price (occasion of sin, source of a thousand very grave temptations. We must be prudent, we are no holier than Adam). I am praying with my whole heart and asking our Lord most earnestly to let you escape military service. He forbade the Jews to return to Egypt after having delivered them from it; I implore him to help you, to uphold you, to direct things in such a way that you will not have to go back into the Egypt of the world from which he has so mercifully brought you out! I pray for you with all that is best in my heart and beseech the holy Spirit to take charge of the matter. Thank you for your excellent letter of 1 October; it was a joy to get it. Thank you. All for Jesus, dearest brother, isn't that so? May his name be perfectly sanctified in you, in us, in everyone! Amen.

Br Charles of Jesus

Dom Louis de Gonzague died suddenly on 3 December 1899, aged 45. Well before then he had become reconciled to Charles de Foucauld's hermetic way of life as references in letters to his brother show: 'As for [Fr Marie Albéric], he is very seriously becoming a true saint. I have never known such a fine soul on this earth' (8/11/1897), and: 'The news of our solitary in Palestine is good; he always prays for N.D. des Neiges and its dear inhabitants' (12/6/1899). Charles de Foucauld received news of the death from Fr Jérôme on 29 December and immediately wrote letters of condolence to Fr Jérôme and Dom Martin. The one selected is to Dom Martin to whom he had not written for so long.

Convent of Poor Clares,
Nazareth (Turkey in Asia),
29 December 1899 *(to Dom Martin)*

Most venerated and beloved Father: Did this have to happen to drag me out of my silence? I received the tragic news this morning and you must know how moved I feel, Reverend and dearest Father. On 16 January it will be ten years since I first arrived at N.D. des Neiges, and it was nine years ago this December that I came under the wing of the good and excellent Fr Louis de Gonzague: memories of his virtues, of all I saw him being and doing, of what he has meant to me and everyone during these nine years, come flocking vividly to my mind and I cannot restrain my emotion and my tears. You knew him better than anyone, you who noticed in him above all that absolute integrity of intention. As he had 'the single eye', let us hope that now 'his whole body is bathed in light'. At times I weep at the memory of his warm affection, his fatherly heart, his virtues; at times I smile as I tell myself that after such a life, and helped by so many prayers and masses, he is already in the fatherland! We shall say a lot of prayers for him in Nazareth; tomorrow and the following days we shall have as many masses as it has been possible to arrange - every day for some time to come several priests will celebrate for that dear soul, but I hope he will smile at our prayers and have no need of them. He spoke a lot of you in his last letter; he was going to come and see me; I was expecting him from day to day. I feel even nearer to him now than when he was on earth; I no longer need to tell him I love him; he sees it; that is the sweetness of solitude, it separates on the surface but not in reality, for it has never separated me from you, from the living, and it brings union with the dead.

You surely know what a large part of my heart I left at N.D. des Neiges, and you must know too that not writing does not mean not loving. Give my news, but without telling them where I am (so as to avoid letters and talk, so that no-one will write to me or discuss me - my news being silence, the hidden life, entombment), but telling them that I love them with my whole heart and pray for them daily, to dearest Fr Eugène, to little Fr Louis de Gonzague, to Br Norbert - these are not the only ones that have a place in my heart though they come first: I would have to make a long list of names - Fr Geniez,[2] Brs Alphonse, Sébastien, Moise, Joachim, Fr Marie, and so on - because everyone at N.D. des Neiges is close to my heart.

From you, beloved Father, I have nothing to hide. Since my arrival in the Holy Land I have become a servant, or rather a labourer, a day-labourer, with the Poor Clares at Nazareth; I have the independence of a labourer, working in my own time and accepting only the work I want, like Mary's workman-son. I organize my time so as to earn my bread honestly and the rest of the time I spend in front of the blessed Sacrament. The Poor Clares (they are so good, real sisters for me, their kindness touches me to the quick; God feeds me on milk) provide me with work and for payment give me not money but everything I need - lodging and everything else. I never go out of the convent, I live an enclosed life and keep the silence; it is God himself who has led me as if by the hand into this haven which he seems to have prepared for me. I cannot praise him enough for what I have found here: recollection and a retreat, and the poverty and abjection of a labourer I have wanted for so long. So now you know all about my very simple life which is becoming more and more hidden.

I commend you to God, to Jesus, venerated and beloved Father! The cause of my letter is sad indeed, but it will come to all of us sooner or later and I hope for him we love it has already produced incomparable joy: '*Qui seminant in lacrimis in exultatione metent*'. I kneel at your feet; please give a blessing to him who will always be your very humble and grateful child, deeply devoted and loving in the sacred Heart of our beloved Lord Jesus,

Br Charles

Nazareth,
17 January 1900 *(to Fr Jérôme)*

My dearest brother in Jesus: Today I am writing to ask you a favour: the abbess of the Poor Clares has asked me if I know anyone who could obtain the blessing of our beloved Father, the Sovereign Pontiff, for the Poor Clares of the convent in Nazareth. He has already given them one in the past, but they are most anxious to receive it again from that dear and venerated hand - especially as this is Holy Year and the Pope, loved with such filial devotion, is advancing in age. I seem to remember that this is a fairly easy thing to get if one takes the correct steps and pays a fee, so I promised to write to you. Everything seems possible in Rome, dear brother, seeing that I have you there, so please be kind enough to discharge my debt of gratitude towards these dear nuns and (so long as no indiscretion is involved either on your part or mine) ask our beloved Fr General or anyone else you judge suitable for these two blessings, or in any case do what has to be done to obtain them. As for the fee, you can write to my cousin de Bondy and tell her what it comes to; I am writing to her by the same post to warn her and she will send it to you.

But this isn't all. I'm going to ask my cousin to send you a quantity of small crosses and medals, of no value in themselves. What I would like you to do is to get all the crosses and medals blessed by the Holy Father and to get the crosses endowed with the privilege that a certain rank of prelate - a cardinal, I think - has the power to confer, the privilege being that on these crosses one can at any time, in any place, in any condition, do the stations of the cross and gain all the indulgences. And then you will send me all the crosses and all the medals by registered parcel post.

What a lot of material things, dear brother, and yet they are not material as to their purpose because it's principally the souls in purgatory that I have in mind, and also to recall and proclaim in silence the great devotions to the sacred Heart, the holy Family, the blessed Virgin and St Joseph that our Holy Father has sought to foster during his glorious pontificate.

Yet another request: (1) Could you send me, in Latin, the formula of consecration to the sacred Heart as given by the Holy Father - I have it only in French; (2) Are these the litanies of the sacred Heart as approved by the Holy See; if yes, say so; if no, correct them or send me the proper ones. Forgive me for so many requests, and thank you!

I am sure we are both still praying for our dearest Fr Louis de Gonzague. We shall never forget him, as he doesn't forget us. 'Even in the intoxication of divine delights he remembers us', said St Augustine. Death is not separation; rather, it unites; we converse more easily and are more one because we are more in God: it is the beginning, the first half, of perfect heavenly union. When will the day come for our half?

... Here are two pictures of my own composition - the hermit isn't good - one for you and one of Fr Louis de Gonzague de St Isidore whom I do not forget - he has his place in my heart and my prayers ...

Br Charles of Jesus

On 28 March 1900 Fr Eugène died, also aged 45.

Nazareth,
10 April 1900 *(to Dom Martin)*

Most Reverend and beloved Father: Your new grief has caused your child to break his silence yet again. Jesus is testing you, so shall I pity you? And shall I pity our dear and beloved Fr Eugène? No, a thousand times no, neither you nor him. For him it is repose, the fatherland, the port. If Jesus thinks him worthy to be brought to rest eternally on his heart, if he thinks the brave soldier has battled long enough with the trials of here below and the time has come for him to receive his laurels, his crown, to enjoy peace in eternal glory and drink for ever of God and his love, then so much the better, so much the better a thousand times!

And how about you, you must miss this dear friend so much, this second brother, this Gérard;[3] you who are now left like a solitary olive at the top of a branch, as if forgotten on the tree after the harvest; you for whom bereavement, grief, suffering and emptiness are multiplied here below – to you Jesus says: 'Blessed are those who weep!' and your mother, St Theresa, adds: 'Above all, my daughters, never complain when we suffer, for we know full well that great treasures are to be found in suffering!' So I don't pity you; Jesus loves you; he knows what is good for you and gives it to you; this death is 'a gift from the hand of your beloved brother Jesus', as Sister Beatrix Onez puts it. Although I love you with heartfelt filial love, I know that it is no more than a poor man's heartfelt love, whereas Jesus loves you in God. I cannot love you better than by uniting myself with him, than by saying Amen to everything that his heart wants for you. May he be blessed for everything!

This letter of mourning is thus a letter of thanksgiving, venerated and beloved Father. As I see things, we cannot do otherwise than give thanks: '*Benedicamus in omne tempore*' here below while waiting to do so eternally in heaven, as already so many cherished souls are doing who only yesterday were sharing our exile, good Fr Eugène and good Fr Louis and so many others.[4] All our dead put our conversation more and more in heaven. Everything we love is already up there.

God be with you more and more, most Reverend and beloved Father, everything always for Jesus. I kneel at your feet; please bless your humble child who loves you with filial devotion in the heart of our beloved Lord Jesus,

Br Charles of Jesus

Charles de Foucauld wrote two almost identical letters adumbrating the next orientation in his life, one to the Abbot General and one to Dom Martin de Gonzague. The one to Dom Martin is selected, being a little fuller.

To Rev. Fr Dom Martin, Abbot of N.D. des Neiges,
La Bastide (Lozère)
Nazareth,
1 June 1900

Most Reverend Father: In a few days I am leaving for Jerusalem to see the Patriarch, Mgr Piavi, a friend of our beloved Fr Dom Louis de G. to whom he gave permission for the monastery at Akbès when he - Mgr Piavi - was Apostolic Delegate at Beiruth. I am going to ask his authorization: (1) to be known openly in Galilee as a hermit and to wear a hermit's habit; (2) to establish there, if it pleases God, a little brotherhood dedicated to the perpetual adoration of the blessed Sacrament and to the hidden, lowly life of meditation that Jesus led in Nazareth; and (3) for the favour of receiving Holy Orders. As Mgr the Patriarch will need to know about my seven years as a Cistercian, and whether I left the Order as a punishment, I am writing to ask you to send the information he needs to him direct, if you would be so good as to add this kindness to those you have already showered upon me.

I shall write at greater length soon. At the moment I shall confine myself to imploring you to pray for me most earnestly, and at this decisive moment of my life and on the eve of undertaking a work for the love of our beloved Lord Jesus, to commend me to all your community which is so dear to my heart, and particularly to those to whom you know I am attached by more special links of charity in the heart of Jesus, little Fr Louis de Gonzague and Br Norbert first and foremost.

I kneel before you, most Reverend and beloved Father ...

Br Charles de Foucauld

V
Notre-Dame des Neiges and the priesthood (1900-1901)

The overture to Mgr Piavi failed, but Charles de Foucauld's desire to receive Holy Orders persisted and after a great deal of negotiation he returned to Notre-Dame des Neiges with this in view, arriving on 19 August 1900. As soon as the arrangements for his ultimate ordination had been made, he went to Rome on business for the Poor Clares.

Rome,
1 September 1900 *(to Dom Martin)*

Reverend and most venerated Father: The journey was excellent and I would have written sooner but that I wanted to give you an address. The Father General of the Trappists is away, as is everyone else I know in the Order. I then went to the Capuchins but their Father General, the only person who can help with my affairs, is also away for two or three weeks and I absolutely must await his return. But I shall not waste my time. God has protected me with his customary goodness throughout my journey and has enabled me to find a professor at the Roman College in whom I have absolute confidence, he has given me a list of authors to go through for my theology before my ordination and then read in depth afterwards. In the absence of their General, the Capuchins have given me loving hospitality, but only for four days; I haven't found any lodgings to go to afterwards, but I'm writing to you all the same so that you won't be worried at not hearing from me; as soon as I have a definite address, at the latest tomorrow, I'll let you know. I hope for a niche next door to the Fathers of the Most Blessed Sacrament so that I can enjoy exposition of the blessed Sacrament during the day; it will be a good place to ponder the mysteries that our Lord Jesus came to reveal and which I am studying for him alone. So don't write before hearing from me again; this should be very soon.

Thank you a thousand times for all you've done for me and continue to be and do. Really I would prefer not to thank you, for my thanks are so far below what I owe and feel. But thank you has to be said all the same, despite my total incapacity, my inability to express myself; I pray our Lord to give me at least a grateful heart. At any rate you must realize that I love you as a son ...

Br Charles

P.S. Don't be surprised if you receive letters from the nuns at Loretto addressed either to Br Marie Albéric or Br Charles de Foucauld, or even to you. As I was embarrassed to broach the subject with them and obliged to conceal the purpose of my visits, I said I was a familiar of N.D. des Neiges and gave them alms asking them to pray for you and your monastery. Will you kindly forward any letters that come from Loretto because they could be important.

Br Charles

Rome,
4 September 1900 *(to Dom Martin)*

Most Reverend Father: My address is Charles de Foucauld, c/o Madame Maria Bassetti, via Pozzeto 105, 3rd storey, Rome.

I'm very well lodged (better than with the Capuchins, better than anywhere else in Rome); I am in a quiet little place prepared for me by God; it is next door to the Fathers of the Blessed Sacrament who found it for me. They have exposition of the blessed Sacrament day and night and I benefit by their chapel as much as if I were living in their convent. The house is very pious, very decent; I can treat it exactly like home which means I can follow my routine as a hermit. I am studying dogmatic theology so as to have some idea of a good half of it by 1 November. I can't see at all at the moment how long I shall be here; the Father General of the Capuchins is not yet back; at all events it will take some time; but it will be easy to come and go: from one point of view Holy Orders has priority over everything, on the other hand it is essential for me to do all I can for the Poor Clares' work which is also God's work and urgent. I am well placed here for my preparation: absolute solitude, continuous silence, no external distractions, a very pious environment, access to any books I want. I have found two good counsellors, a professor at the Roman College and a professor at St Anselm's College - it seems an unhoped for and special protection that God should have given them to me at this time of year. My only course, it seems to me, is to stay here for the time required by the Poor Clares' affairs, perhaps returning once, or even twice if necessary, to N.D. des Neiges for a week or a fortnight. I know this involves movement and money but I don't see any other way of managing, unless it pleased God to smooth out the difficulties and cut things short - which would be so easy for him. Please ask Br Norbert to pray for me to do God's will, and remember me religiously to Frs Louis de Gonzague, Aurèle, Hermann, Augustin and so on as well as to Brs Norbert, Augustin, Moise, Toussaint, Sébastien, etc. ...

Br Charles

I have received through the Capuchins a letter from Abbé Huvelin. I don't know if he sent it direct or if he sent it to N.D. des Neiges and you forwarded it to the Capuchins; if you forwarded it I notify you of its arrival and thank you very much. Don't send me any money, dear Father, I don't need it; if I need some later on I shall tell you so in all simplicity.

Br Charles

Charles de Foucauld arrived back at N.D. des Neiges from Rome on 29 September 1900 and stayed at the monastery for a year, passing through all the stages that led up to his ordination to the priesthood on 9 June 1901 (Corpus Christi). As N.D. des Neiges lay in the diocese of the Bishop of Viviers, Mgr Bonnet, it was in the seminary chapel at Viviers that ordination took place in the presence of Mgr Bonnet and Dom Martin. Charles de Foucauld knew that on his return to N.D. des Neiges his sister, Madame de Blic (whom he had seen only once in twelve years), would have already arrived for his first mass the following morning so he had left this note in her room:

Darling, thank you for coming, your arrival touches me deeply. I shall get back on the night of Sunday/Monday at about midnight or one in the morning; so just wait for me, but go to bed early like the Trappists who go to bed at eight. As soon as I get back I shall go straight to the church and to the Blessed Sacrament to whom my first visit is due; and I shall remain in silence and adoration until after my first mass. You won't be able to speak to me before my first mass but we shall make up for it afterwards, darling; the community mass is sung at half past 6 in front of the blessed Sacrament exposed; I shall be deacon. As soon as this is over I shall go to the sacristy, put on a chasuble, and re-appear at the same altar to say my first mass; I shall give you holy communion through one of the grills of the little chapel where you will be. After my thanksgiving (three-quarters-of-an-hour or an hour after) I shall come and pay you a really good visit. Wait for me in your room at that time. Mind you have a good breakfast after your communion. Make sure that your coming here is a real joy for the whole community who are full of illusions about me and love me a thousand times more than I deserve, and especially the good Fr Abbot who is coming to Viviers on purpose to be with me despite his many occupations. Welcome, darling, and thank you for coming. I embrace you as I love you - with all my heart in the heart of Jesus,

Br Marie Albéric

Meanwhile his plans for the final period of his life had been taking shape - the long Sahara period for which he is most widely known. These plans were best expressed, not to a Trappist brother, but to an old friend of pre-Trappist days, Henri de Castries, in the following letter:

The Monastery of Notre-Dame des Neiges, par La Bastide, (Lozère)
23 June 1901

My dear friend: The silence of the cloister is not the silence of forgetfulness. More than once during these twelve years of blessed solitude have I thought of you and prayed for you. I was delighted recently to have good news of you through my cousin Louis.

It is for God that I have kept silence all this time and it is for God that today I break it. There are one or two of us here who cannot recite our Pater without thinking with pain of the vast spaces of Morocco where so many souls live without 'sanctifying God, forming part of his kingdom, doing his will or knowing the divine bread of the holy Eucharist', and as we must love these poor souls as ourselves we would like, with God's help and despite our littleness, to do all we can to bring Christ's light to them and enable the radiance of Jesus's heart to shine on them.

With this in view, and so as to do for these unfortunate people what we would want done for ourselves were we in their place, we want to found on the Moroccan border, not a Trappist house, not a big rich monastery, not a centre for agricultural development, but a sort of humble little hermitage where a few poor monks could live on fruit and a little barley harvested with their own hands, in a narrow enclosure, in penance and adoration of the blessed Sacrament, not going outside their enclosure, not preaching, but giving hospitality to all comers, good or bad, friend or enemy, Muslim or Christian. It is evangelization not through the word but through the blessed Sacrament, the mass, prayer, penance, the practice of the evangelical virtues, charity - brotherly and universal charity that shares the very last mouthful of bread with any poor person, any visitor, any stranger, and welcomes every human being as a beloved brother.

What place should we choose for attempting our little foundation? - that is to say the place most favourable for the good of souls, where relations can be formed with the Moroccans, the place best situated to form a wedge, a breach, for future penetration to the border by which Morocco is most accessible to evangelization. I think it is the south. Thus it seems to me that we should establish ourselves on some *solitary* oasis between Ain-Sefra and Tuat. We would give humble hospitality to travellers, to caravans, and also to our soldiers. We fear neither hardship nor danger, on the contrary we love them and hope for them. No-one knows this region better than you: this is why I am writing to you, to ask you to be so kind - you who have always showered kindnesses upon me - as to do me yet another favour and tell me what point in the extreme south would seem the best situated for our first little settlement.

I commend our humble project to your prayers, you who love Algeria and Morocco. I beg you to believe in my very respectful and devoted affection. Your humble servant in Jesus,

Br Charles of Jesus
(Charles de Foucauld)

Notre Dame des Neiges,
17 July (1901) *(to Fr Jérôme)*

Dearest Father: What a joy to write to you after this long silence, and how lovely it will be to receive your news, to see by your letter, and to hear from Fr Henri,[1] that you love Jesus more and more, which is the one thing needful.

You have been constantly in my thoughts and prayers during this long silence. Silence, you know, is just the opposite to coldness and forgetfulness: *in meditatione exardescet ignis*. It is in silence that we love most ardently; noise and words often put out the inner fire; let us be silent, dearest Father, like St Magdalen, like St John the Baptist;

let us pray God to kindle within us the fire that made their silence and solitude so blessed. How they must have loved! ...

I have written at length to Fr Henri and asked him to show you my letter, so you will see what the life of my soul has been, what my desires and plans are, where I think my duty lies despite my unworthiness and incapacity. If I depended on myself my plans would be mad, but I depend on God who said, 'If anyone wants to serve me, let him follow me'. He said 'Follow me' so often and told us to 'love your neighbour as yourself, do for others what you would wish them to do for you'. It's impossible for me to practise this precept of brotherly love unless I devote my life to doing all the good I can do to those brothers of Jesus who lack everything because they lack him. If I were a Muslim knowing neither Jesus nor his sacred Heart, nor Mary our mother, nor the holy Eucharist, nor the bosom of our holy Church, nor the gospels, nor any of the things that constitute our happiness down here and our hope up there, and if I were aware of my tragic condition, oh how I would long for someone to come and get me out of it! And what I would wish for myself, I *must* do for others: 'Do for others what you would wish them to do for you', and I must do it for the poorest, the most abandoned, the most lost sheep, I must share my feast, my divine banquet, not with my rich brothers and neighbours (rich in the knowledge of things unknown to these unhappy people) but with the blind, the crippled, the beggars, a thousand times more to be pitied than those who suffer only in their body. And I don't think I can do them a greater good than by bringing Jesus to them as Mary brought him to John's house at the Visitation; Jesus, the good of goods, the supreme sanctifier; Jesus present among them in the tabernacle and, I hope, in the monstrance; Jesus offering himself on the holy altar every day for their conversion; Jesus blessing them every day at Benediction; here lies our good of goods, our all, Jesus; and at the same time - in silence, not by words but by example and above all by universal charity - I would try to show our ignorant brothers what our religion is, what the Christian spirit is, what the Heart of Jesus is.

Pray for me, dearest Father; you see how much your unworthy brother in Jesus needs your prayers; he counts on them; and as for you, you will always be in my memento till the last mass of my life, as you were in the first. I was ordained priest on 9 June and said my first mass the next day. And where are you up to in your studies and orders? You must have made your solemn vows a year ago and the sub-diaconate must have followed. Write a long letter giving your news, dearest Father, you can imagine how welcome it will be after this long silence which has grieved me; it will be sweet to see your handwriting again ...

Br Charles of Jesus

VI
Sahara, first period: Béni-Abbès (1901-1905)

Charles de Foucauld left Notre-Dame des Neiges on Friday, 6 September 1901, having been there for a year. He left alone (despite the 'one or two of us' mentioned in the letter to Henry de Castries). He disembarked at Algiers on Tuesday 10 September and almost at once wrote to Dom Martin.

(no address or date) *(to Dom Martin)*

Beloved Father: The parting from you on Friday was more painful than I can say. How often have I thought to myself since your final blessing that if I were seeking consolation in this world I would never leave the community of N.D. des Neiges where I have such a dear father and such loving brothers. It goes without saying that I love you yourself most of all, but I don't love only you; there is no monk, novice or lay-brother in the community for whom I do not feel the most tender affection; if they are not altogether perfect (I'm not a judge and don't know about this) they are and always have been entirely perfect for me: there isn't one who has not showered kindness, affection, delicate attentions and brotherly love on me: I was as it were the spoilt child of the community; they vied with each other in courtesies, favours and devotion. Tell them, please, how grateful I am and that they are entrenched in my heart and my prayers. *You* must tell them, I cannot myself, I am utterly incapable of expressing what I feel. Also please commend me to their prayers, I love them all with my whole heart.

When I got off the boat I found Mgr Guérin[1] and good Fr Henri waiting for me on the quay. They both greeted me with touching kindness. You don't have to spend half an hour with Fr Henri, as you said: three minutes are enough! Mgr Guérin has granted me all the necessary authorizations. I shall telegraph you today asking you to send all the luggage to the harbour-master at Algiers, addressing it c/o the White Fathers at Maison-Carrée so that the notification of delivery shall reach me. I shall leave for the south just as soon as the luggage has arrived and I have obtained the necessary authorizations from the military authorities. If you haven't yet dispatched the luggage when this letter arrives then wait for a case from Paris (monstrance, ciborium and so on) so that everything can come together. Thank you in advance. I have chosen to set up house at Igli, an oasis 300 kilometres south of Figuig. Pray that I shall be faithful. Jesus never fails me but I'm afraid of failing him: pray for your unworthy child.

On my way to and from Sainte-Baume I was received with incomparable kindness by the Fathers of the Most Blessed Sacrament. They gave me the most affectionate hospitality. I prayed as well as I could for you and my dear brothers of N.D. des Neiges. I was very glad to have gone there.[2]

Embrace all my brothers for me. It seems pointless to name one more than another when I love them all so much. Yet Br Augustin, Fr Frédéric, Br Moise and Br Germain have a very special place in my gratitude, my heart and my prayers: tell them so. But the one who has the most special place of all, beloved Father, is you to whom I owe so much, to whom I owe everything, and whom I loved with all my heart even before I was so indebted to you. Bless from afar your humble and unworthy child ...[3]

Br Charles of Jesus

P.S. I shall leave for the south as a priest free to give religious aid to our soldiers, without mentioning a convent or anything like that to the military authorities;

the rest will come into being little by little without any noise in the way Jesus wants. Send me companions if Jesus shows you suitable ones.

Maison-Carrée, Monday, feast of SS Cornelius and Cyprian
16 September 1901 (*to Dom Martin*)

Beloved Father: I hope to have all the military authorizations for my departure as well as the recommendations to facilitate my journey between the 20th and 25th. I've already received the ones from Mgr Guérin. So, if it pleases Jesus, I plan to leave for the Sahara at the beginning of next week. If you want me to get information about Tunisia or southern Oran, let me know at once. I had a letter from M. de Castries today indicating Belghari in the Gourara oasis (between Timmimoun and Deldoul) as being very propitious for a Trappist foundation. It's a small oasis, isolated, abandoned, with water, where, he says, a large palm-grove could be rescued and re-made; things would be safe there because the oasis, though isolated, is surrounded on all sides, if at a distance, by points occupied by our troops. If you or Fr General would like to set about starting something there it would be easy.

Mgr Guérin is leaving for the Sahara. The few days that will elapse between his departure and mine I shall spend at Staouéli. I asked Fr Henri if this would be possible and he had the goodness to say yes, so send any letters or parcels to Staouéli.

You are constantly in my thoughts and my prayers. You know how much I count on the prayers of my fathers and brothers and most of all on yours. Commend me to the prayers of all of them but especially to those of Br Augustin, Br Moise, Fr Frédéric and Br Germain. If you find a soul among them that you believe before God is called by Jesus to follow me, send him quickly. That's what I most need. The question of a server at mass will be a huge problem once I've gone south, a problem on the first day and every day. The missionaries have numerous faculties but not the one of saying mass without a server; I am asking Jesus for one and pray St Magdalen to choose him and send him to me. If you find a soul capable of being a good religious, prepared to follow me, ready to face martyrdom, to die of hunger and obey faithfully, send him to me, if you think it is Jesus's will.

The White Fathers' kindness has filled me with confusion and gratitude. Whether concerning Tunisia or the south they can provide you or Fr General with priceless information supposing either of you wanted to start a house here ...

Br Charles

Staouéli,
2 October 1901 *(to Dom Martin)*

Beloved Father: As you probably know, the government has told the Algerian authorities officially that the law concerning congregations (contrary to the formal assurances previously given) is also applicable in Algeria.[4] Thus Algeria is in exactly the same situation as France so cannot serve as a refuge in case of need. Tunisia already is or soon will be in the same situation as Algeria. I thought I had better tell you this in case you weren't absolutely clear as to what the position was.

I plan to leave here any day now, perhaps tomorrow, but please go on sending everything to Staouéli in a double envelope, putting Fr Henri, Prior and so on, on the top one.

If you find anyone who you think may be sent by God to accompany me, send him to Fr Henri first. A companion is what I most need, I cannot even celebrate holy mass without a Christian server; what shall I do? Jesus will provide if it is his will and if I am not unworthy. Pray for my conversion, that's the main thing. Tell all my dear and excellent fathers and brothers to pray for me; commend me to the whole community and especially to Br Augustin (his good angel should surely send him to me, if it is Jesus's will).[5]

Mgr Livinhac[6] has told me that in Uganda (which can be reached easily now because of the new railway) where the blacks (who are of Abyssinian race, that is to say Copts) are already excellent members of religious orders and there are many conversions despite the four-year period as neophytes imposed on all and the stiff instruction they have to receive, and where they would make very good monks and certainly provide vocations to Trappist monasteries from the start - in Uganda, which is in English territory and under the jurisdiction of the White Fathers, the White Fathers would receive and welcome Trappists with open arms and hearts and would help them to the utmost of their ability. Land can be bought at one franc twenty-five centimes (1F 25c) a hectare, and this land is so fertile that five men working not too hard can feed twenty. I've written all this to Fr General but have told absolutely no-one else but you two. It could be a refuge; the people are so well disposed that they come to the missions 1000 or 1200 strong solely to receive instruction. At this moment there are 60,000 Catholics and 120,000 neophytes in the vicariate ...

Br Charles of Jesus

(no place or date) *(to Fr Jérôme)*

Dearest Father and brother in Jesus: I have just a moment to let you know what a great consolation it was for me to see you again. I praise Jesus for having given me this unhoped-for joy. How good God is: he gives us unexpected crosses for the greater good of our souls which we in our cowardice can hardly accept, and at the same time gives us joys which are all the sweeter for being less hoped for. Dearest Father and brother, the cross, the cross, the cross, let us seek with our whole heart the pure and naked cross, Jesus's cross - in obedience always, naturally - and let Jesus take care of the consolations he thinks we need; he doesn't forget, and will give us sweeter ones than we ourselves would dare to ask for.

Obey your superiors and confessors, God's representatives for you when he says, 'He who hears you, hears me'. This is the means of always being guided by God himself, as well you know. I beg you to pray for this sinner who prays for you and loves you with his whole heart in the heart of Jesus.

Br Charles of Jesus

Béni-Abbès,
3 November (1901) *(to Fr Jérôme)*

Dearest Father: I think of you every day and shall think of you most of all tomorrow. You have your place every morning in the memento of my mass which you have served so often, and you will have it especially tomorrow on St Charles's day,[7] our common feast. Nor do I forget those dear to you - I pray my best for them.

Please thank Jesus for the protection he has given me: with his divine power and sweetness he has smoothed a path that seemed fraught with obstacles. He so arranged things that I should obtain with no difficulty all the ecclesiastical and military authorizations I needed; that I should make the complicated and expensive journey to Béni-Abbès free of charge; that I should choose without previous knowledge this wonderfully propitious place for my settlement; that I should get the hermitage and chapel built at no cost when I thought it would be far too expensive for my slender resources; and that I should be welcomed by every sort of person, officers and men, Christians and Muslims, a welcome that fills me with confusion and gratitude and makes it easy for me to try to help them.

Pray for your humble and unworthy brother, dearest Father, that he may not be unfaithful to all these graces, that he may love God and men as the Heart of Jesus would have him do ...

Br Charles of Jesus

Béni-Abbès,
5 November 1901 *(to Dom Martin)*

Beloved Father: Here I am, after a splendid journey, at the place chosen for my settlement. May Jesus be praised for everything! I am filled with confusion and adoration at seeing how he has arranged things and smoothed out all difficulties. Pray that I may do the good that is to be done here, that I may be faithful - the more graces I receive the more wretched I see myself to be and the more fearful of being unfaithful. I am having an oratory built with three cells and a large room for receiving visitors: the nearest dwellings are about half a mile away, far enough for me to be alone, yet near enough for their inhabitants to be able to come to mass and exposition of the blessed Sacrament. The officers and men are competing in kindness towards me and have been good enough to serve my mass up till now. My chapel and the cells and so on will be finished in two or three weeks at the most, I think; in the meantime I have a very suitable room for celebrating holy mass (with *your* ornaments, *your* chalice, *your* missal, in fact everything coming from you, which I never forget). I'm going to rent a small plot of land if possible for growing potatoes.

I never forget you, beloved Father, nor all your dear religious. I pray my best for them; commend me to their prayers ... I am thinking a lot about the young fathers and how you can get them out of military service: if I can think of any way I'll let you know, but at the moment I cannot see any certain way of getting them out of it entirely; here, they would only do one year, of that I'm sure, but I'm trying to find a way of sending them to a place where the law dispenses them entirely ...

Br Charles of Jesus

You can write to me direct at the following address: Br Charles of Jesus, Béni-Abbès (extreme south Oran), Subdivision of Ain-Sefra, Province of Oran, Algeria...

6 November. I've reopened my letter to tell you that God has just granted me the immense and unhoped-for grace of obtaining at a very reasonable price a large fruit garden and kitchen garden with a good yield, enough to occupy and in some years feed 8 or 10 monks - they form a single entity with the chapel and the cells and in a few weeks all will be encircled in the same enclosure. Furthermore the enclosure will be easy to enlarge. It is a great grace for which I thank Jesus.

Béni-Abbès,
6 December 1901 *(to Dom Martin)*

Beloved Father: Thank you for your note of 17 October and for little Fr Louis de Gonzague's letter of the same date. I'm writing just a line today to share my joy with you. Since 2 December the most blessed Sacrament has been in the little tabernacle made by Br Romeuf, lined with silk by Fr Ildefonse and Fr François, blessed by you, and housed in the little chapel that Jesus has caused to be built of bricks dried in the sun and palm-tree trunks. On 30 November (St Andrew) I took possession of the chapel of the 'fraternity of the Sacred Heart' of Béni-Abbès; the following day the first mass was said in it and on the 2nd the blessed Sacrament was installed. Pray Jesus that I serve him faithfully, that his will may be totally done in me, in my brothers if he sends me any, in all the faithful and infidel souls in this region, and in all men ...

(Unsigned)

Béni-Abbès,
23 December 1901 *(to Fr Jérôme)*

So now you're a deacon, dearest Father, and I pray Jesus to make you a holy deacon, totally wrapt in the holy Eucharist which you now have the immense happiness of touching, totally engulfed in Jesus whom you now see so close on the altar. A happy Christmas for everyone and for you and me, for you who are drawing so close to our Lord, for me who for the first time will see him born in my hands: it will be my first midnight mass! It overawes me to think of it! The first Christmas mass at Béni-Abbès and (very probably) the first in this region - I'm overawed by that too! We certainly need to pray for each other, dear Father, that you may be a good deacon, a good monk and soon a good priest, and that I too may be faithful to grace and do everything that Jesus asks of me.

I am very near you in these blessed days, the first of your diaconate; I see you on the altar, taking the ciborium from the tabernacle, placing the sacred Host in the monstrance, carrying the monstrance, infinite delights that the angels would envy you were they able to envy! How happy we are! But how unworthy we are! Let us try to be faithful, let us pray and work to become so, let each pray for the other.

Here there is much to be done, for natives and officers and men: there are 200 Christian soldiers, very many natives, most of them poor, many poor travelling Arabs; alms, hospitality, charity, kindness, can do a great deal of good among the Muslims and dispose them to know Jesus. A lot of good can be done for the soldiers too: I hope some of them will go to communion at midnight mass, I hope to be able to draw them to me so as to draw them to Jesus.

A happy Christmas and a happy and holy year, dear Father. Your name is with me every day in the memento of my mass; I am praying for you more than ever in this period which is so full of graces for you, and I shall do so particularly at Christmas at that blessed midnight mass. Soon it will be your turn to celebrate the holy Sacrifice; you should prepare yourself for it by being more and more faithful to daily graces, more and more engulfed in the one and only beloved, Jesus.

Thank you for your excellent November letter. I haven't yet received the parcels so carefully wrapped up by you - as soon as they arrive I'll write: thank you for taking so much care for my sake! May Jesus reward you.

I'm writing no more than a note today, dear Father, because I am so busy. There's no-one but myself for all the work of the monastery; these early stages, and especially the approach of Christmas, keep me very occupied: we shall have exposition of the blessed Sacrament from 6 a.m. till 6.30 p.m. on Christmas day and perhaps even from midnight till 6.30 p.m. I am so happy about this. Jesus has so visibly blessed this little foundation of Béni-Abbès that I shall never be able to thank him enough and am desolated at not being more faithful. Thank him for me, dear brother in Jesus, and beg him to make your humble and unworthy brother in Jesus faithful, your brother who loves you in the heart of the one and only beloved Jesus.

Br Charles of Jesus

Béni-Abbès,
30 December 1901 *(to Dom Martin)*

Beloved Father: A happy and holy year to you and all your dear community. I pray for you with my whole heart, and for Akbès, and for Frs Fabien and Arsène. I shall say three masses for each of them.[8]

Thank you for your welcome letter of 1 December. Thank you for the powers for apostolic indulgences; very affectionate thanks to good Fr Aurèle and please remember me to him most respectfully. Thank you for your offer made once and for all of board and lodging at dear and blessed Notre-Dame des Neiges. I promise you I shall never forget it and shall take advantage of it should the need arise, as I have done unhesitatingly in the past. Thank you, beloved Father, with all my heart. Yes, your house is mine through my love for it and through the charity and forbearance for your wretched servant and son that exist there. Thank you for the mass intentions; at the moment I can manage without them so think it more perfect to do so, following my rule. But if ever, and it may be soon, I am in need of mass stipends I shall let you know. You can send them by money order; I shall find a way of cashing it.

May Jesus bless Fr Placide's desires and make of him

a humble, fervent and holy religious. The date 1 January is a blessed one for good Br Augustin; please give him this picture and embrace him for me.

Jesus is showering graces on me. There was exposition of the most blessed Sacrament at Christmas from midnight to 7 p.m. - a small number of soldiers were in constant adoration. I hope with God's grace that there will be exposition again on 1 January from 7 a.m. till 7 p.m. Enough soldiers come to church for me to read a passage from the holy gospel and give a little talk. After this instruction, which lasts about 20 minutes, there is benediction of the blessed Sacrament and evening prayers. What a grace - daily benediction of the blessed Sacrament, exposition, and a nucleus of good souls! Pray God that I shall be grateful and faithful.

The natives give me consolation too; an average of 75 come every day to ask for alms: a little barley, the problem is to have enough barley; others simply come to see me. All are very well disposed.

I shall do good - or rather God will do good through me - insofar as I am holy: and I am a sinner. Pray God for my conversion, and ask the whole community that I hold in my heart to pray for the conversion of its unworthy brother in Jesus. I pray with my whole heart for Mgr Bonnet and all the diocese of Viviers. When you see him beg him to bless me from afar and remember me in his prayers.

Christmas night, midnight mass, the three Christmas masses, all made me think of you so much and pray for you. It is to you and to Mgr of Viviers that I owe all my blessings, after Jesus. My deepest gratitude and most devoted tender and filial love belong to you, beloved Father, as you know. As soon as I have found some way of helping your young men in the matter of the three years I shall let you know; it is constantly in my thoughts ...

Br Charles of Jesus

Please pray for the abolition of slavery here. It thrives as in the first century of the Christian era, and under the protection and with the approval of the French government; it is horrible! May Jesus bring a remedy! Advise me! How must I deal with this horror? Ask Monsignor's advice on my behalf.

Béni-Abbès,
9 January 1902 *(to Dom Martin)*

Beloved Father: I'm writing on this paper not only for love of our divine Saviour's poverty and his crib, but also because the superscription on the envelope will please you: your son's poor dwelling and oratory are beginning to be called the fraternity by Christians, Muslims and Jews; moreover this envelope is a precious souvenir of today which is one of the most blessed days of my life, for today I have been able to ransom a slave for the first time, if not without difficulty; with the help of St Joseph, to whom I entrusted the matter, I was able this evening to restore his freedom to a poor young boy from the Sudan who was snatched from his family four or five years ago. The Captain to whom I entrusted my purse sent me in this envelope the statement of the price agreed on by the master of 'Joseph of the Sacred Heart' (the name I have given the freed boy); on these grounds this cheap envelope is a sweet souvenir for me. I wanted to tell you about this grace received from God so that you could thank him for me and make good by your thanksgiving the inadequacy of my own.

I have received your fatherly letter written on Christmas Eve. Thank you with all my heart.

The freeing of Joseph of the Sacred Heart has left me broke and even in debt, so send me mass intentions after all. If I receive any other money between now and then I shall send them back to you; if not, I shall keep your money and say your masses. Always send money by postal order (not by registered mail); not only can I cash it but it's the only quick and practical method of getting money: registered letters take two or three months.

You did absolutely right to take in Fr Placide. I would have done the same *'Beati misericordes'*. It's in this way that you resemble your Father who is in heaven... I still have no companion: *mea culpa! mea maxima culpa!* I am not worthy...

Br Charles of Jesus

Béni-Abbès,
3 February 1902 *(to Fr Jérôme)*

Dearest Father: My whole heart and all my prayers go out to you in your great sorrow, and I shall pray my very best for your dear departed father. But there is a heart much closer to yours than mine, and much closer to his, and that is the heart of our beloved Jesus. May we hope for all the mercy that his divine heart can bestow! If his heart is so bountifully merciful towards all men, then how much more merciful must it be towards the father of a monk and a nun? We must hope and pray. 'Charity believes everything, hopes everything'; if we must 'believe everything and hope everything' of men, then how much more must we do so of God?

Today we shall have exposition of the blessed Sacrament all day; the blessed Virgin gives me this grace for the feast of her purification; I assure you that your father shall not be forgotten as I kneel before Jesus; he will have his good share of my poor and unworthy prayers, and my next mass will be for him. Dear Father, I am sorry for you, but only moderately so, because Jesus tries those whom he loves, and the trial he has sent you proves his love for you, his plan to make you more and more holy; nothing sanctifies like suffering. You must benefit by your present sorrow to make yourself more perfect; you must pray a lot while hoping a lot; 'all is possible to him who prays'; if we must hope for the salvation of your dear father's soul from 'the heart that so loved men', then we must do for that soul what we would like to be done for us, and hasten its entry into the divine presence if it is in purgatory. The potency of our prayers is proportionate to our goodness, 'God listens to his friends', Jesus wants this sorrow for you not only to make you more perfect by destroying everything in you that is human imperfection, but also to be a spur driving you to sanctification so that you may do good to the soul that has given you so much - oh, so much - for, after God, you owe him your being, your education, your faith, that is to say eternal life, almost!

May Jesus watch over you, sanctify you, make you profit by this ordeal in the way he wants. I embrace you as I love you, beloved Father, with all my heart in the heart of Jesus.

Br Charles of Jesus

With this letter the correspondence with Fr Jérôme comes to an end; if other letters were written they never reached the archives of N.D. des Neiges. Fr Jérôme was the only correspondent among his Trappist brothers whom Charles de Foucauld treated as a pupil rather than as a mentor or an equal (naturally enough, as Fr Jérôme was twenty years his junior), and this gives the correspondence a special interest. Fr Jérôme left the Trappists in 1909 to become a secular priest which he remained, working in Algeria, until his death in 1962.

Béni-Abbès,
7 February 1902 *(to Dom Martin)*

Beloved Father: Heartfelt thanks for your letter of 23 January received last night. I see now that there's an easy way of getting a quick answer from you: asking for money. Thank you for the 40 francs for the 40 masses *pro defuncta Maria.* I'm very touched that you should help me like this when you yourself are so poor. And thank you for the stamps, and thank you still more for your full clear answer about slavery. What you say is what I do with the slaves I personally meet: far from preaching revolt and escape I preach patience and hope, I say God permits your hardships for your improvement and your glory in heaven, pray to God and sanctify yourselves, 'seek first the kingdom of God and all the rest will be added to you', man's slavery and his earthly home will soon pass, like life, think of Satan's slavery and the eternal Fatherland.

But, having said that, and while consoling them as much as I can, I feel my duty isn't yet finished, I feel I have either to say myself, or get the law to say, '*non licet*'. '*Vae vobis hypocritis*' (woe unto you hypocrites), you who put liberty, equality, fraternity and the rights of man on your stamps and everywhere else, then tighten the chains that bind your slaves; you who condemn to penal servitude those who fake your bank notes, then allow children to be snatched from their parents and publicly sold; you who punish the theft of a hen, then allow the theft of a man (in fact nearly all the slaves in these parts are children born free and taken violently from their parents). Moreover we must 'love our neighbour as ourselves' and do for these wretched people 'what we would wish to have done for ourselves' - 'see that none of those entrusted to us by God shall be lost', and he has entrusted us with all the souls in our territory. We must not meddle in temporal government, no-one is more convinced of that than I, and yet 'we must love justice and hate iniquity', so when the temporal government commits a grave injustice against those in our care (in our care to a large extent - I am the only priest over a length and breadth of 300 kilometres in this prefecture) then the government must be told that this is what it is doing, for it is we who stand for justice and truth in the world and we haven't the right to be 'sleeping watch-men', 'dumb dogs', or 'careless shepherds'.

So (though we are both in full agreement as to how to behave with the slaves themselves) I am wondering whether it is not my duty to raise my voice either directly or indirectly in order that France may know about the injustice and condoned slavery in our lands; whether I ought not to say or cause to be said: This is what is happening, '*non licet*'.

I have informed the Apostolic Prefect - perhaps that is enough. Far be it from me to want to start talking and writing, yet I don't want to betray my children, I don't want not to do for Jesus what he needs as living in his members. It is Jesus himself who is in this tragic situation - 'what you do to the least of these my little ones you do to me'. I don't want to be a bad shepherd or a dumb dog. And I'm afraid of sacrificing Jesus to my love of peace and quiet and my innate cowardice and timidity ...

For the first time I understand St Gregory the Great's laments for the loss of the peace and quiet of the cloister, though I truly believe that I want only what Jesus wants when I see myself as a man of words and ministry (while never leaving the enclosure): but my guests - the poor, my slaves, my visitors - never leave me alone for a moment; I am on my own for all the duties of the monastery; ever since the 15th when the little guest house was completed there have been guests for supper, bed and breakfast every day, not counting a cripple who is here all the time; I usually have between 60 and 100 visitors a day. So you see how much I need a companion, but a tried companion. If you think it might be Br Augustin's vocation to join me, then this is the time to send him; he can now have a regular life here, and if he can be satisfied with little more than bread and water he will not die of hunger, and anyway I am ashamed of these last words and ask Jesus's forgiveness for we know that 'to him who seeks the kingdom of God and its justice all the rest will be added'. Your young fathers are still constantly in my mind, but I don't see a way of getting them out of military service certainly and totally; as soon as I think of anything I'll let you know. I hope it will be soon ...

Br Charles of Jesus

Béni-Abbès,
17 March 1902 *(to Dom Martin)*

May Jesus sanctify his name in you, beloved Father.
Venerated and beloved Father: Heartfelt thanks for your

letter of 25 February. It gives me strong proof of your deep affection and touches me greatly. Let me reassure you by telling you that I have put everything into the Apostolic Prefect's hands, I have told him all about the situation and asked him to act as he sees fit (which is what I meant when I said I thought I had done enough by telling him). Where I do not agree with you is that I think you resign yourself to evil too easily. You resign yourself too easily to a state of affairs that is ruinous for souls.

But as for what I personally should do, I think, as you do, that I should inform my Apostolic Prefect and then abide by what he says. My position allows me to see very well that I could easily do more harm than good by following another course. So that is what I have done. I have taken the necessary steps to inform the Apostolic Prefect of the facts, and I have told him I shall do nothing except on his orders; but I don't think he will give me any orders - for the very good reason that it is easier for them to act than me; they can do things very well by themselves.

I shall have to ask you for more mass intentions, beloved Father. The freeing of that child - who is now a Catholic catechumen and in Algiers - has ruined me, so that despite my reluctance I shall have to fall back on mass intentions to pay for my piece of land. Thus I would be very grateful if you could send me some. Forgive me for making such demands on your poverty. Jesus will repay!

This letter will reach you at Easter, and I do not forget that at just about that date a year ago you led me up to receive the diaconate. I join my alleluias with yours, I sing with you: *Resurrexit sicut dixit, alleluia*! *Regina coeli laetare, alleluia*!

Br Charles of Jesus

Béni-Abbès,
24 April 1902 *(to Dom Martin)*

May the name of Jesus be sanctified in you and in

everyone. Beloved and venerated Father: Many thanks for your excellent letter of 3 April and for the 40 francs. How good of you to share your daily bread with me! But don't send any more mass stipends until I ask again because I've just received a wonderful present with which I've been able to pay off my plot of land completely; I now owe nothing and so, once I've said your masses (which are very useful for giving me something in advance over a long period) I shall stop receiving mass stipends following my rule. Thank you for the pictures too, dear Father... I am feeling with you deeply in your family loss, beloved Father, and am praying for you and yours. We must hope. 'Charity hopes everything'.

If your nephew turns up here as a sergeant in the engineers you may be well sure I shall give him a brotherly welcome and shall not - voluntarily - fail either to show him my affection or let him profit by the presence of Jesus under our roof. But you haven't told me his name. Let me know his name, and meanwhile I shall be on the look-out for sergeants in the engineers; I'm sure he can't have arrived yet for no captain in the engineers has yet come to see me.

I deplore even more than you the three years' military service for your children. If you would like to send some of them to me for ten years they would certainly do only one year of service and perhaps even none - because everyone is so kind to me. But you would have to send them to me as laymen under the title of gardeners; or if they were priests then in black cassocks under the title of sacristans; it's humble, yes, but if they don't want to humble themselves then Jesus doesn't want them and nor do I. Moreover they must be prepared to die of hunger (I can feed them only on barley gruel, sometimes with sour milk added, and who knows whether there will always be barley, though I have never lacked for anything yet) and have their heads cut off...

If you send me someone, send him first to Fr Henri at Staouéli and he will send him on; but you must send someone who feels called to remain with Br Charles for always, or else one of your children for a number of years so as to escape military service; in either case the following three conditions must be fulfilled: (1) they must be good religious and above all obedient (or disposed to be so); (2) they must be prepared joyfully to die of hunger and lack everything for Jesus; (3) they must be prepared joyfully to have their heads cut off for Jesus.

My land is paid for. It comprises about 9 hectares, plenty of water, 180 palm trees and quite a few other fruit trees; there is enough to occupy and feed twenty to thirty monks in cultivating the fruit trees and doing the garden; it's enough for them to live on because the number of palms can be increased and their yield is good. On the 16th, the feast of St Benoit Labre, I started the enclosure wall that will entirely encircle the property; I build for five hours a day but I am a *very* mediocre mason: no statement of mine will you find it easier to believe.

In a few weeks I hope to receive a visit from the Apostolic Prefect whom I love with all my heart.

Don't you think you would obtain a little glory for Jesus if you sent me someone, for as soon as I have just one zealous companion I shall be able - thanks to the authorizations and faculties provided by the Apostolic Prefect - to have exposition of the blessed Sacrament for quite a few hours *every day*. Pray for my conversion, that is the only thing I really need. For 'to him who seeks the kingdom of God all the rest shall be added' ...

Br Charles of Jesus

Béni-Abbès,
15 May 1902 *(to Dom Martin)*

Most venerated and beloved Father: I cannot let the feast of the Sacred Heart and the anniversary of my ordination come and go without coming as a son to put my wishes at your feet and my deep gratitude - gratitude greater than I can express, but less than the favour received, because what you placed in my hands is infinite, it is Jesus himself whom you entrusted to my mean and wretched hands. Thank you with all my soul, beloved Father, and never enough; never enough as you yourself must admit. And happy feast-day. It's the feast of all of us because it's the feast of the heart of our Beloved, our Spouse, our All; *Deus meus et omnia.* If only we could be lost in this divine heart! What I wish for you on your feast is that you may not live any more but that He may live in you. So it's death that I wish for you. And I wish I could share it! How I long to die like that and to die in all the ways that glorify Jesus!

If Br Augustin feels the same as he did when I left N.D. des Neiges, then you ought to send him to me; in all conscience it seems to me God's will. Here, as almoner and gardener, without any temporal occupation that has to do with the world, in the great calm of the desert, he would be able to put his immense charity into practice in the distribution of alms - hospitality (very elementary) to the wandering natives, remedies to the poor natives - while work in the garden would bathe his soul in that peace which is the fruit of simple, moderate, regular manual labour, and his piety would be nourished by exposition of the blessed Sacrament for several hours a day (a grace that his presence would provide). I would have, I already have, enough to feed him. The chapel, the sacristy, a guest-room are finished, two more large rooms will be completed in a few days. I am in the process of building the enclosure (1,500 metres round) and am being as good a mason as I can be. I owe nothing, the property is all paid for. Jesus is blessing this humble work; in fact it lacks only two things - brothers, and myself: by myself I mean my conversion, because my conversion would attract brothers. You are waiting for my conversion before sending me Br Augustin; you don't trust me. In this you are right, I am a miserable sinner, guilty every day of a hundred examples of cowardice, infidelity, lukewarmness, so pray for my conversion on this feast of the Sacred Heart, procure it from the heart of Jesus, commend it on that day most earnestly to the prayers of the community. Then reflect seriously, and ask Jesus if it is not his will that you send me Br Augustin. I believe it is (unless this brother's inclinations have altered since last year). It is in any case a good thing that he didn't come at the beginning; both for his sake and the foundation's it is better that I started out alone; he wouldn't have had enough peace in all the commotion of the early days; a lot of things were more easily done by me alone than by me accompanied. But now that the arrangements are sufficiently advanced for him to have silence and meditation, I think the moment for his coming has arrived. My reasons for thinking so (always assuming his feelings have not changed) are as follows: (1) he could have the sort of life that suits his soul better here than at N.D. des Neiges: wide benevolence, the exercise of charity, humble manual labour; (2) his presence would permit of exposition of the blessed Sacrament for eight hours a day - an inestimable grace; (3) his exceptionally beautiful soul is of the type God uses for the foundation stone of his edifices; (4) before he knew me, before he became a Trappist, he wanted to enter a monastery in the Sahara, in Tuat, and had there been one there he would have entered (so the attraction is one of long standing and hence remarkable).

As for myself, all I want is that Jesus's will shall be done; how could I want anything more when I have the blessed Sacrament? I would indeed be difficult, not to say mad, if I lacked for anything. When I began my letter I hadn't meant to talk about Br Augustin, but for some time now I've been reproaching myself (seeing it as an example of my cowardice) for not doing so, and it relieves me to have explained my views so fully; it was a duty to Jesus and a duty to the good brother.

Pray for my conversion: that is what I lack, the only thing I personally lack, but it's a great lack! Every day at mass and at benediction of the blessed Sacrament I pray with the best of my heart for you, beloved Father, and for all my dear brothers and fathers. I shall discharge the three masses for brother Jean-Baptiste...

Br Charles of Jesus

Béni-Abbès,
8 September 1902 *(to Dom Martin)*

Most venerated and beloved Father: It is just about a year since I left not only your cherished roof but you yourself, most blessed and cherished of all. The day before yesterday evening it was a year since I made my confession to you and received your final blessing and then left for the station with your children and my brothers, Fr Frédéric and Fr Germain. However far away my body may be, beloved Father, my heart is always with you. Every day at mass and at evening benediction I pray for you and the dear community I love so much, where I feel so loved and so at home, where I have twice found such a marvellously fatherly roof. I thought about you so much on the eve of St Bernard's feast-day, and about my arrival at N.D. des Neiges two years ago, about your welcome, and my time there, and about my priesthood which I owe to you.

Thank you for everything, beloved Father. I hope I didn't distress you by saying all I did about Br Augustin. I felt it my duty to write to you in that way because I told him when I left that he should follow your advice unreservedly and obey you blindly, so I owed it to him, to *him*, to write to you as I did; I felt it was my duty - if I was mistaken, then God forgive me. In any case you must realize that I don't depend on Br Augustin, much as I love him in Jesus, nor on any living soul, nor on myself, but only on Jesus. If this little family of monks I have in mind - living in poverty and adoring the blessed Sacrament in missionary countries - is destined to come into being, then it is for God to found it, not for men: 'every plant that the heavenly Father has not planted will be torn up'. I'll be the very first not to want it if Jesus doesn't want it, though I continue to believe that my duty consists in living according to this rule and in doing all I can so that others may come and join your child.

My life is always the same: a life according to rule.

I am still alone.

I see a lot of people; yet my life is not diversified or troubled or dissipated by continual visits - it is animated. People knock at my door more often that at yours: slaves, guests, the poor. The brotherhood now consists of the chapel, the sacristy and three big rooms. Seven tall crosses which are my joy rise up from seven mounds six foot high dominating our property and showing that Jesus has taken possession of this bit of land.

Jesus is in the holy tabernacle as he has never ceased to be since first he entered here. I have said holy mass every day, I have never been ill. I'm thinking of you so much during these current persecutions. Let me have news of you, the community, the Order...

Br Charles of Jesus

As to Dom Martin's reluctance to send a companion to join Charles de Foucauld we have a clue in a letter he wrote to Mgr Guérin, Apostolic Prefect of the Sahara, round about this time:

You exhort me to send him an assistant, a companion. At the moment I cannot and even if I could I would still hesitate. As you know, Monsignor, my admiration for the heroic virtues of Fr Albéric is immense, and based on a friendship of twelve years. The only thing that amazes me is that he doesn't work miracles. Outside books, I have never encountered such holiness on earth. But I have to admit to having reservations regarding his prudence and discretion. The austerities he himself practises and would certainly impose on his companions are such that I cannot but think a neophyte would very soon sink under them. Moreover the intense single-mindedness that he imposes on himself and would impose on his disciples seems to me so superhuman that I fear he would drive a disciple mad by excessive mental concentration before killing him by excessive austerities. However, if you think we could send someone without endangering his life, I am prepared blindly to fall in with your decision and shall try to find a companion as soon as possible.

Years before, when Charles de Foucauld was still at Akbès, Abbé Huvelin had written to him: 'You are not made, **not at all made,** *to lead others'.*
That hope sprung eternal in Charles de Foucauld's breast is proved by a letter that he himself wrote to Mgr Guérin in June 1908: 'I shall write by the same post to the Father Abbot of N.D. des Neiges to ask him to lend me Br Augustin for a year - a lay brother, a former Zouave, tall and oh so good - you must have noticed him. By his charity and gentleness and prayers, by the example of his manual labour and his warm and loving heart he would do good. He would certainly do good, so I shall ask for him. I am not frightened by the possibility of a refusal'. There is no trace of this letter to Dom Martin.

Feast of St Theresa,
15 October 1902 *(to Dom Martin)*

Most venerated and beloved Father: Thank you for your excellent letter of 3 September. I have chosen the feast of our mother, St Theresa, to tell you how much I am with you and praying for you. At mass and at benediction of the blessed Sacrament I always pray very particularly for Mgr of Viviers, my bishop, and you, my father, and for all your spiritual children - his diocese, your monastery.

I am very touched that the good and holy Mgr Guérin has been to see you. He has told me your news by letter as I shan't be seeing him for two or three months.

I am enclosing a photograph of our first baptism at Béni-Abbès: the child is Abd Jesu (Servant of Jesus), a name often used in Syria and Palestine in the early Church, a little negro of three-and-a-half who will go as soon as possible to the orphanage run by the St Vincent de Paul nuns in Algiers where they expect him. I'm sorry that that elderly monk had to be with him[9] but it was the only way of getting the photograph. Pray for the sergeant-major who took it and lovingly gave it to me.

I am still alone. May Jesus's will be done. Pray for my conversion - it's my mediocrity that stops people from joining me. 'Unless the grain of wheat dies, it remains alone'.

Béni-Abbès as a danger zone is an invention of the newspapers or a manoeuvre of the government. Everything here is calm.

Pray for my conversion, pray for the people all around me - all these hosts of people in the process of losing their souls; these poor unfortunates have every vice because the devil prevents them from opening their eyes to Jesus's radiance and therefore has no difficulty in dragging them into sin.

I am happy spiritually: very solitary.

And happy materially: poor for myself, but rich for the poor (I get a fair amount of presents given me on purpose for them).

I am living in community with Abd Jesu and another negro (a catechumen aged 14 provisionally called Paul), a ransomed slave as is Abd Jesu and, like him, going as soon as possible to Algiers...

Br Charles of Jesus

Béni-Abbès,
25 January 1903 *(to Dom Martin)*

Most venerated and beloved Father: Many thanks for your two letters of 1 December and 1 January. How can I thank you for what you've done for M.D., for sending him 40 francs; I'm so touched and thank you with all my heart. I have an impression he didn't go and see you after receiving them. In fact I've had a very unfavourable account of him, it seems he is married but has left his wife and child: we do what we can for souls: the seed often falls by the wayside or on stony ground or among thorns: thank you for what you did for him.

And thank you for the news of your soldier children: may Jesus bless them. But oh, you must do what you can to spare them this peril: I've recently been in touch with some monks and seminarians doing their military service. Alas, alas, there's nothing to say but alas: of course there are some who stand up to the test but for many it is disastrous.

Monsignor will be rewarded in heaven for what he's suffering on earth in Jesus's service. Persecution by Nero and by the Synagogue led St Peter and the apostles and Jesus himself into heaven: by persecuting God's children these wretched people are weaving their crowns while preparing hell for themselves.

Try to send me some brothers. I've now got one Christian and three catechumens. What I would like to have, if Jesus will build it, is a little Christian village; but I cannot make it alone; I have the children or young people to look after and I also have to adore Jesus in silence; lots of things need to be done and someone on whom I can absolutely depend seems indispensable. Yet if he really were indispensable, then I would have him. Nevertheless I feel I must do everything in my power to procure him. There is exposition of the blessed Sacrament for at least eight hours every day: two people are always in adoration. Pray for my conversion: lazy, greedy, idle, lukewarm - such is your unworthy child. Now I am going to take you into my confidence about two things, this is just between ourselves; help me if you can, not through your own means in the matter of money, but through others if you can interest them in this work. I need two things, first, companions (my plot of land, once cultivated, will be able to feed 25 monks in four years) so that good may be done, so that Jesus may be adored, and so that, little by little, spreading like an oil stain or rather like a fragrant perfume, we may enter Morocco and there plough a deep furrow (Morocco is my goal): I must have companions both so that the community of Béni-Abbès can be formed and so that we can found settlements in Morocco in the name of the heart of Jesus (whose flag floats over the brotherhood every day during exposition of the blessed Sacrament). The second thing I need is money so as to be able to ransom slaves. As in the early Church it is the slaves who are the first to open their hearts to the gospel, but they can't possibly be converted or found a Christian village while remaining in their masters' power; as soon as their masters (these are mainly nomads with flocks in the desert) see that they come and listen to me they pack them off to tend flocks in distant places and don't let them come near me again; so no possible conversion, nor instruction, nor marriage, nor founding of a Christian village. They must be ransomed, they must be set free. Not all of them, but those that one knows or hopes are disposed to become good Christians. If you come across anyone who could and would help, please think of this, as also about companions.

Pray and get others to pray for Morocco: it is my goal. Silent communities could be set up there fairly easily with God's help, and they would open the way for others. And why don't the Trappists start a foundation there? The government would probably favour such foundations because it needs to increase the number of its dependants in Morocco. And then it's so near: from Marseilles it's so cheap to get to Tangier or any of the Moroccan ports, and the land around the ports is very fertile and very healthy. Good vocations would be plentiful from the Spanish side which is so near, without counting the others. The postal service is good; everything invites; and everyone forgets.

Pray for the conversion of Morocco and get others to pray for it. And pray and get others to pray for mine.

You would have given great pleasure to my cousin de Bondy had you been to see her on your way to Ciron. She would have liked to go to Fontgombault, all the more as she knew you were there, but she was ill so couldn't. I assure you that any visit of yours would always give her enormous pleasure. And it's a real act of charity to give her this consolation for she really is beset with every kind of trouble; it must be hard to bear as many crosses as she bears, and such heavy ones.

Commend me, as well as Morocco and the Sahara, to the prayers of all my dearest brothers and fathers...

Br Charles of Jesus

Béni-Abbès,
23 May 1903 *(to Dom Martin)*

Most venerated and beloved Father: Very many thanks for your letter of 3 May. I'm particularly glad to get it because in my ignorance of everything you could have been expelled and already far away without my knowing. I am thinking about you so much in these turbulent times but I'm not afraid for you because you are in Jesus's hands. If you are suffering, the cross on earth will be a crown in heaven. Get one or other of the fathers – Fr Germain or Fr Frédéric for instance – to write often and keep me in touch so that I may know whether or not you are still at N.D. des Neiges.

In a few days it will be the anniversary of my ordination. I shall celebrate it with such deep gratitude to you, beloved Father. How vividly will you be present in my memory! What a large part you will play! What a large part you *did* play! Only two years ago; how short a time! You know I love you and that my heart is filled with gratitude. Can gratitude add to love? I would like it to, but I don't know...

Br Charles of Jesus

At this time the Congregation for the Propagation of the Faith in Rome ('Propaganda Fide') wrote to the Father General of the Trappists asking for particulars concerning the ordination of Charles de Foucauld (P[adre] Carlo di Gesù, visconte di Foucault, as he is referred to). Father General asked Dom Martin to write in answer, which he did (22/12/1903), and the second half of his letter deserves to be quoted here:

Six months after his ordination to the priesthood, with the consent of Mgr of Viviers and Mgr Livinhac, superior of the White Fathers, he was accepted by Mgr Guérin, Apostolic Prefect of the Sahara, and started his ministry in that prefecture.

I do not know his official title but in practice he is

chaplain to the French camp near Béni-Abbès in the province of Ain-Sefra, south Oran. On account of his learning, his outstanding holiness and his admirable charity, he is doing an amazing amount of good in those regions.

He has great influence with the officers, especially the superior officers, some of whom were his fellow-pupils at St-Cyr; as for the men, they have already canonized him. His holiness is so dazzling that it is apparent to everyone: as for the Arabs, they venerate him as the most saintly and the most hospitable of priests.

He arrived at El Moungar 48 hours after the battle was over: he gave the last sacraments to all the wounded (48, I think). *Not one of the wounded died.* At N.D. des Neiges, where we believe Fr Albéric to be a saint, we think that this could well be a little miracle on the part of our former brother. It is indeed extraordinary that among so many wounded, all so ill-tended, far away from doctors, from pharmacies, from hospitals, and in such an unhealthy climate, not one of those horribly mutilated men died.

Very Reverend Father, if you could obtain the goodwill of the Sacred College of Propaganda for our saintly friend of Béni-Abbès, you would be doing a work that is very pleasing to God...

The following letter to Mgr Bonnet, Bishop of Viviers (which, though not addressed to a Trappist brother, is also in the possession of N.D. des Neiges), should be quoted here as being the first to show that Charles de Foucauld was again on the move:

Adrar (Oasis Sahariennes, by Béni-Unif),
28 May 1904 *(to Mgr Bonnet)*

Monsignor: It is a long time since your unworthy child knelt at your feet. Since 16 January I have been on the move as a missionary monk; a visit was required to the natives of the newly-subdued south, no other priest was free to make it, I asked permission to do so, this was granted, so here I am, on the road for the last four months and likely to be so for three or four more.

My heart, my thoughts and my poor prayers never leave you; my travels do not prevent me from celebrating holy mass, and every morning, while offering and adoring the divine victim, I beg him to pour out his best graces on my beloved bishop and on the dear diocese of Viviers which adopted me.

In my travels among the natives I am sometimes without news of France for quite a time; at the moment I have received none for over two months. The thought that Jesus might have permitted you and your diocese and N.D. des Neiges to be submitted to new ordeals that I know nothing of makes me pray for you with increased urgency and emotion. I pray my very best for you to the heart of Jesus.

The feast of the Sacred Heart and Corpus Christi (the anniversary of my ordination) bring even more vivid memories of you than usual; I cannot express my heartfelt gratitude to you who made a priest of my unworthy and wretched self. Dare I ask you to crown the kindnesses you have already done me by praying for me that I may be faithful; the harvest is so great! At the moment I am the only labourer in this vast field, and I labour so badly! I beseech you to pray Jesus for me and for all those poor natives of Morocco and the Sahara who, alas, are engulfed in the shadow of death! *Cor Jesu sacratissimum adveniat regnum tuum!...*

Br Charles of Jesus

On the road (with the nomads)
Ascension, 1 June (1905)[10] *(to Dom Martin)*

Beloved and most venerated Father: I received your letter of 30 April some days ago and also Brother Augustin's.

I have prayed Jesus, Mary and Joseph to lead you to do for Akbès what they would do in your place, what the heart of Jesus wishes, and I shall go on praying to them in this sense. I have no special illumination on the problem. '*Non sum dignus*'.

My advice is that Notre-Dame des Neiges should take back Akbès as her daughter and so preserve the life that she gave her, but to this end she must do three essential things: (1) give her a good superior; (2) do some much-needed weeding-out of personnel; (3) take measures to ensure that the poverty of Jesus be practised both at Akbès and at Notre-Dame des Neiges so that there will be no serious increase of expenses for Notre-Dame des Neiges.

The reasons for this advice are as follows:

(1) A monastery is a very important thing, a place where there is a tabernacle, where the blessed Sacrament is reserved, where the holy Sacrifice is offered, where the canonical office is recited, where the evangelical virtues are practised and where souls in a state of grace consecrate their lives to the love of Jesus.

(2) It is an especially important thing in the infidel countries where altars, tabernacles, the faithful, saintly souls, are so rare!

(3) It is an outstandingly important thing at Akbès where the monastery, situated as it is between Muslims, schismatic Armenians and lukewarm Catholics, is well placed to enlighten the first, bring back the second and strengthen the third, and to help the Schismatics and Catholics not only to become good Catholics but to become good monks (which has already happened).

(4) It is an outstandingly important thing at Akbès where the monastery, having relations with the Lebanon and the Maronites among whom slack monks abound, can have and inevitably will have (in proportion to its zeal) a very happy influence on the Maronite monks (which has already happened).

(5) When Leo XIII gave an audience to the superiors of all the Trappist monasteries, he tapped the superior of Akbès on the cheek saying, 'Bravo Syria!' None of the others received this encouragement. The Holy Father, understanding Syria's needs, gave special encourage-

ment and approval to Akbès, so if we want to share the opinion of that great Pontiff then Akbès must be carefully preserved.

(6) We complain of the ravages caused in France by ungodly hands. So let us not cause them by our own in countries where religious houses are much more necessary than in France, because unbelief is still much more general there and servants of Jesus much more rare.

(7) I see no possible reason for abandoning Akbès. The monastic virtues can be practised there as elsewhere, as witnessed by your brother, by good Fr Polycarpe, Fr Philomène, Br Dominique, Br Julien and so many others. One can live by monastic work there as elsewhere and better than in most places: the monastery lands are vast, the soil excellent, water abundant, work in the fields easy; there better than elsewhere even can you live the saintly monastic life: the place is very isolated, the site imposing and full of memories: twelve miles from Tarsus, twenty-four from Antioch which can be seen in the distance, it is full of memories of the apostles and the crusades. Far from France, far from the family, far from public news, one is well placed for forgetting the world and looking only to God. Then inspiration is derived from the memory of the holy monks whose bodies are there awaiting the resurrection, Fr Louis de Gonzague, Fr Polycarpe, Fr Philomène and the others. The feeling is strong that Jesus's words are being fulfilled: 'Go out into the world and teach the gospel to everyone'. It would be hard to find anywhere so favourable to the monastic life, whether for the inner life or for the easiness of living by manual labour.

But let me repeat that while feeling so strongly, so absolutely, that there is every reason for N.D. des Neiges to take back Akbès as a daughter and so preserve her life, it is indispensable that N.D. des Neiges should provide her with a good life and hence do three things: (1) give her a good superior; (2) instal a good community formed of souls of goodwill; (3) see that poverty, the poverty of Jesus, of St Bernard, is practised both at Akbès and at N.D. des Neiges so that taking back Akbès does not add financial strain to N.D. des Neiges.

Beloved Father, here we are at 1 June; on the 9th it will be the anniversary of my ordination, on the 10th of my first mass. How my heart and all my thanks go out to you! Forgive me for expressing myself so badly, forgive me for my short letters. I have faith that you believe in my filial love and my gratitude.

My work is overwhelming. I am again on the road, as you see, and will be so for months...

Br Charles of Jesus

The monastery of Notre-Dame du Sacré-Coeur at Akbès continued its life until 1915 when Turkey entered the war beside Germany and the monks, nearly all French, left for another monastery so as to avoid internment. An effort to revive Akbès after the war was short-lived; it was raided by bandits in 1920 and the last remaining monk, refusing to leave, was crucified on an improvized cross and left to die.

VII
Sahara, second period: Tamanrasset (1905-1916)

The correspondence with Dom Martin now comes to an end. If there were other letters during the next few years they must have perished in the fire at N.D. des Neiges in 1912. Nearly all the remaining letters are to Br Augustin, to whom reference has often been made.

(Tamanrasset),
25 July 1907 *(to Br Augustin)*

My heartfelt thanks for your excellent letter, dearest brother; it has just reached me in the Hoggar where I shall remain till the end of the summer. From late March until early July I was travelling among the Tuaregs with hardly a break.[1] But for three weeks now I've been back in my hermitage in the Hoggar, settled in again, enjoying afresh the presence of the blessed Sacrament and finding this regular life very sweet after so many months of travel. Regular life indeed: my solitude enables me to live as in a monastery, but a monastery where I am brother porter, but brother porter with not many visitors, the poor asking for alms, the sick asking for cures, but only a few of either. Thank you, dearest brother, for your excellent letters (please go on remembering me!) and for the good wishes of so many dear fathers and brothers. Tell them I pray for them all every day, and ask them to pray a lot for me and for the poor Tuaregs, Moroccans, Saharians, Muslims of every colour. And you especially, beloved brother, pray a lot for them and for me, you to whom I am so deeply, so fraternally devoted *in corde Jesu*...

Br Charles of Jesus

Tamanrasset by Insalah,
5 March 1908 *(to Br Augustin)*

Beloved brother: I have just received all together your four letters of 15 September, 10 December, 20 December (enclosing 300 francs) and 15 January. Heartfelt thanks for them all and also for the 300 francs which I would never have received but for you and which comes at just the right moment. How good you are to pass the hat round for your brother. I shall write to M. Jorrand to thank him.

No, I wasn't with our troops in Morocco; whoever said that was mistaken. I would have been very pleased to be there, but I wasn't sent for, and as I am here without news (I have just now received six months' mail) I can't do anything unless I am informed and arrangements are made for me to follow our troops. Without news and without being asked for I stayed here and shall do so all the summer. I have decided not to return to Béni-Abbès until November, spend the winter there, then come back here in the spring.

You ask for information about the Hoggar. It's very high. I am at an altitude of about 4,600 feet and even at that I'm only at the foot of the central range which is over 6,500 feet at its lowest points and about 10,000 at its highest.

There are streams, but not many; water is under the ground rather than at the surface, but it abounds - in lots of places you only have to scratch the earth to find water. The rivers don't flow except for a few days after the rains, but they always have water to a depth of three or four feet beneath the river bed, which makes it possible to divert their waters to cultivatable land and grow cereals.

The Hoggar is small; 150 kilometres from north to south and the same from east to west. The centre is very mountainous, too stony, too cold to be cultivated, but the border, where I am, is surrounded on the lower slopes by a string of hamlets which, taken together, bring in on an average 70 tons of wheat, 25 tons of barley and 40 tons of millet, which is good for the Sahara. The winter is cold but snow is rare. No wild animals. The summer is lovely: the temperature as in Nantes or Tours.

How can I thank you for the precious relics of the Curé d'Ars? They are treasures for the Hoggar and will bring his prayers and Jesus's blessing to it and me. And thank you for your beautiful pictures which touch my heart all the more as they correspond to my great desire for devotion to the Holy Spirit and St Magdalen. And thank you for the beautiful verses on St Magdalen.

I am enclosing two little pictures, one for you, one for your dragoon. Yes, I do know Colonel Laperrine very well, we were second lieutenants together in the African light cavalry in south Oran; I love him and admire him very much. As with all honest men, it's better not to beat about the bush so I'm sending him your letter and your nephew's and telling him to do what's best. You are not unknown to him; he knows how much I would have liked to have you with me. I've been telling him about you for a long time now.

I hope it may be possible, but I don't really think that the Colonel can ask for him; most likely your nephew must first put in a request to go into the Arab department and, once there, must try to get himself sent to the Saharians and I shall try to help. I'll send you Colonel Laperrine's reply as soon as it comes.

I love you with all my heart *in corde Jesu,*

Br Charles of Jesus

Tamanrasset by Insalah (via Biskra-Ouargla)
Whitsunday 1908 (8 June) *(to Br Augustin)*

Dearest brother: Many thanks for your welcome letter of Easter Monday. I have just received it thanks to the newly-organized postal service between Insalah and Gao through the Ahaggar and the Adrar. And thank you for the precious relics and for the picture of our father St Joseph. I like receiving relics in the Ahaggar; they're the first steps in taking possession; they sanctify the country; they make one hope that the saints to whom the relics belong will say special prayers for it.

I've had no answer yet from Colonel Laperrine about your nephew, and I couldn't have had one because my letter reached him when he was on a trip far away from here and he cannot write to me; but I shall be seeing him in a month and we shall talk about your nephew then. In any case he may have communicated with him direct so as to tell him what course to follow. This course is: the Arab department. Your nephew has only to put in a request for the Arab department to have the moral certainty of getting into the Saharian Company of Tidikeit after a relatively short time, for in spite of this Company's great advantages it isn't very much sought after because many men, alas, prefer the comforts of the north to nights spent under the open sky and days of marching under the hot sun.

Thank you for the news of everyone. I pray for all the dear fathers and brothers at N.D. des Neiges and particularly for Fr Frédéric, Fr Germain, Fr Placide, Fr Antonin, Br Toussaint, Br Moise, Br Pierre de Cordemois, and so on - all, in fact, as I love them all with my whole heart. Commend me to their prayers and commend also the Muslims of the Sahara. Let them pray for them while waiting for conditions to improve and they come and found a Trappist monastery among them. It is a country's duty to evangelize the infidels in its colonies just as it is a parent's duty to send his children to catechism class. No-one in France seems to have an inkling of this duty. The four million Muslims in Algeria are totally neglected. Explain this duty to our good fathers and brothers and ask them to discharge it by prayer, which is all-powerful, while waiting to discharge it by founding a monastery.

Béni-Abbès would be excellent for twenty monks: I would willingly make them a present of my hermitage.

Try to convince them of this duty, one which everyone in the nation should compete to fulfil; and make them pray...

Br Ch. of Jesus

Dom Martin died on 11 December 1908 aged 52. Though young himself, he had already outlived several august contemporaries and, as Charles de Foucauld put it, was 'like a solitary olive at the top of a branch, as if forgotten on the tree after the harvest' - a somewhat premature harvest, as Fr A.Robert aptly remarks.

Insalah,
12 January 1909 *(to Br Augustin)*

Beloved brother: I have just arrived at Insalah and found your letter with the tragic news. Poor Brother Augustin, how lonely we both are! How lonely we both would be if Jesus were not so close, so beside us, so within us! And our beloved father is also near us, nearer, much nearer than if he were here below, even for you, so how much more for me.

Yet despite this union with uncreated love, despite this union with our dear and good father - a union so much greater than before - the grief remains and we feel all alone in the world, deprived of the one who was so loved.

May Jesus be praised for everything. He has given his reward, granted entry into the fatherland, to his faithful servant; and within the vision of eternal charity, within the heavenly union, his servant loves us so much more than before, he sees us all the time, hears us, protects us.

I'd like to go on and on talking about him but it's impossible at the moment. I've just arrived at Insalah; the mail goes out tonight. And I too am setting out, to El Golea. I've only got half a day to answer the whole mass of letters I found here.

I cannot tell you how utterly touched I am by your sending me the pectoral cross of our beloved and venerated father; I'm enclosing a line to Fr Placide to thank him. This token of remembrance touches and moves me to the depths of my heart, as do also the hair and the bit of rope. Thank you for all the mementoes, and the relics, and those of Fr Ginhac and the Curé d'Ars. And thank you for your letters of the 6th, 12th and 22nd. Tomorrow I shall be utterly with you and my mass intention will be that Jesus shall give Notre-Dame des Neiges the abbot that will glorify Him the most.

I embrace you as a very sad brother and a very much consoled one; I embrace you even more tenderly than usual, as a brother embraces a brother when they have just lost their father, and what a father, but a father who is certainly in heaven.

My thanks to all the community for their messages and prayers...

Br Ch. of Jesus

Between El Golea and Mzab,
2 February 1909 *(to Br Augustin)*

Beloved Br Augustin: Heartfelt thanks for your letter of 31 December, and for your prayers and wishes. I pray for you with all my heart and for all the fathers and brothers at N.D. des Neiges.

It is not impossible that I may be obliged to go to France for ten days at the end of February. In that case I would like to stop for a few hours - between trains - at N.D. des Neiges which is my mother, and at Viviers where is my father. Please be so good as to ask Fr Abbot[2] for permission for me to spend a few hours at N.D. des Neiges if I go to France. Answer without delay c/o M. Eugène de Blic, Villa Fragonard, Grasse (Alpes Maritimes). And please tell me at the same time whether or not Monsignor is at Viviers. It goes without saying that if I go to France, and visit you, I shall let you know the exact date in advance...

Br Ch. of Jesus

This trip took place and Charles de Foucauld arrived at

N.D. des Neiges one day in February. He said mass at the altar of the Blessed Virgin, served by Br Augustin, then visited Dom Martin's grave. In the afternoon he addressed the community in the chapter house and shortly afterwards left to catch his train. Br Augustin accompanied him on the three-kilometre walk to the station.

Grasse,
5 March 1909 *(to Br Augustin)*

Beloved brother: I thank Jesus for having granted me the unhoped-for grace of seeing you again; may this favour make us pray for each other more fervently, may it increase our gratitude towards so good a master, so tender a spouse, may it make us pray for each other's intentions, and serve God's glory and the coming of his kingdom; divine favours should make us produce more and better fruits. May this one have that result, beloved brother. Pray more and more for me and the infidels of Africa, and I shall pray more and more for you and N.D. des Neiges. While praising Jesus for the hours I spent with you, with my whole heart I thank you for them too...

Br Ch. of Jesus

Tamanrasset by Insalah via Biskra,
31 July 1910, St Ignatius *(to Br Augustin)*

Dearest brother: A thousand thanks for your letter of 25 April and the holy pictures and your prayers. I pray my best for you and all the fathers and brothers of N.D. des Neiges. We have certainly had our share of trouble these last few months. On the feast of St Joseph Mgr Guérin, our dear and holy Apostolic Prefect, went to heaven aged 37 after a few days' illness (acute fatigue). My most recent letters from France tell me that my director who has been my spiritual father for 24 years - ever since my conversion - and who has been ill for some time, is now past hoping for. Probably now as I write he has left this world. Pray for these dear and holy souls and ask Fr Abbot and the community to pray for them.

My own little life goes on as usual. I am still alone, to my great regret. I would so love to have a companion who would be my successor - who would pray with me and better than me, be esteemed and loved by the infidels more than I am, prepare souls for the gospel better than I can, set an example of manual labour which would be invaluable to these proud and lazy people, lead a life of monk and missionary, show forth in his life the evangelical life and prepare for the kingdom of beloved Jesus...

Br Ch. of Jesus

In February 1911 there was a second and last visit to N. D. des Neiges

Marseilles,
17 February 1911 *(to Dom Martin II)*

Very Reverend Father: I am so touched and grateful for your kindness in consenting to welcome me at Notre Dame des Neiges. I plan to arrive at La Bastide on the 20th at 3.52 a.m. coming from Nimes, and leave for Paris at 4.6 p.m. the same day. The few hours spent with you and the dear fathers and brothers will be very sweet and I thank Jesus for this consolation.

I kneel at your feet, Reverend Father, and beg you to grant your blessing to your very humble servant who offers you religious and filial devotion in the sacred heart of Jesus,
Br Charles of Jesus

Ch. de Foucauld

Tamanrasset, Algeria,
13 May 1911 *(to Fr Antonin Audigier)*[3]

Dear and Reverend Father: Your letter has found me in

a very remote place where the post comes seldom and slowly - hence the delay in my reply.

You ask me what my life consists of:

It is the life of a missionary monk based on the following three principles: imitation of the hidden life of Jesus at Nazareth; exposition and adoration of the most blessed Sacrament; living among forsaken and infidel peoples and doing everything possible for their conversion.

I am alone, and have been so for ten years. If God grants me brothers it would be better for the salvation of souls - given the vast extent of the infidel areas to be converted - to divide up into small groups of three or four, as many groups as numbers permit, rather than to set up more populous monasteries. Except in very rare cases, when an exception might be made in favour of an outstandingly virtuous man, I would like to have only priests, excellent priests and of mature age.

The life is monastic; perpetual fasting and abstinence, no wine, great poverty, the manual labour of the poor and the peasant, but in moderation; about 8 hours prayer, holy reading and spiritual exercises, 8 hours manual labour or apostolic work, 8 hours for sleep and meals. From the point of view of austerity the life would be more or less equivalent to a Trappist one, less hard in some ways, but much poorer and therefore harder in other ways. For spiritual exercises, the divine office recited together (never sung) without any obligation of choir, adoration of the blessed Sacrament, prayer and holy reading according to preference (or rather according to the indications of the confessor). For manual labour, poor abject work like our Lord's at Nazareth. The superior of each small group of two or three will know the aptitudes, inclinations and needs of his brothers, and according to what he judges to be God's will he will direct them either totally to manual work, or partly to manual work and partly to apostolic work, or almost totally to apostolic work. Apostolic work as I have done it up till now and as I envisage it consists in talking as person to person with infidels (and sometimes with

Christians); the person entrusted with this task here and as things are would be like a Benedictine with four jobs at once - porter, hosteller, confessor for strangers, pharmacist; however there might be journeys to make, the beginnings of a ministry to fulfil.

I see these outposts, these hermitages with three or four missionary monks, as advance-guards designed to prepare the way and then to give place to other religious or an organization of secular clergy once the ground has been cleared.

Comparing this life with the Trappist one you would find a life of equal austerity but much harder because of the greater poverty, and harder too because the climate is hard and tiring and the food completely different from European food: but there must be no question of introducing European food here which would be a costly luxury - our food must be that of the people of the country, corn, dates, milk and its products. As for clothes, as for habitation, you will find only what is poorest and most rustic, nothing resembling the well cared-for clothes and houses that the Trappists have in France, but very much resembling what Jesus's clothes and dwelling may have been like at Nazareth. You will have a different life from the Trappist one in that although everything takes place at its allotted time and following strict obedience, there are none of those little external regulations that Trappists have scrupulously to obey, but just simple family life. You will have a different life from the Trappist one in that there is no sung office, no sung mass, nor any vocal prayer other than the breviary, but much adoration, much silent prayer, much holy reading in front of the blessed Sacrament. You will have a different life from the Trappist one in that some part of the time allotted to manual labour will, if the superior thinks it needful and following his directives, be employed in such apostolic work as he thinks fit.

If God were to send a certain number of brothers we would ask Rome for solemn vows according to the rule of St Augustine, and the name 'The Little Brothers of the Sacred Heart of Jesus'.

At present I am alone; I have four places, four hermitages, in the Sahara, and I go from one to the other; if there were two of us, my brother would be based permanently here, with the Tuaregs, where the constant presence of a priest is more necessary than elsewhere; I would be with him for seven or eight months of the year, and during the four or five others I would be at my other hermitages; if there were three of us, my two brothers would be always here, and I would be here for seven or eight months. If there were more than three or four of us then we would begin to divide up and live in two residences, and so on.

May Jesus's will be done! May his kingdom come!

Anyone wanting to come and join me should first address himself to the Apostolic Prefect of the Sahara at Ouargla (by Biskra) in the department of Constantine. Before granting him definitive authorization to join me, the Apostolic Prefect will probably tell him to spend a few days at Maison-Carrée, near Algiers, the mother-house of the White Fathers, to make himself known to them; and after that, before letting him leave for the Sahara, he will tell him to spend a few weeks, or perhaps a month or two, first at the Kabylie mission and then at a White Father mission in the Sahara so that he may get some idea of the life - *not* the life that he himself will lead which will be very different, but the life of the people he will live among and the ways in which they can be helped.

May Jesus bathe you in his light, dearest Father, may he enable you to be and do what he wants of you at every moment. Ask the same for me. May each of us be and do what Jesus's heart desires; and may it be the same with all souls. *Omnis spiritus laudet Dominum. Fiat voluntas tua sicut in coelo et in terra.*

You may show this letter to any priest who thinks he may be called by God to share my life, on condition that he is exemplary and of mature age.

You humble brother religiously devoted in the beloved heart of Jesus,

Br Ch. of Jesus
(Ch. de Foucauld)

Asekrem by Insalah via Biskra-Ouargla,
24 November 1911 *(to Br Augustin)*

Dearest brother: A thousand thanks for your letter of 11 June. It has taken some time to reach me because since July I have been in the Ahaggar, not in my hermitage at Tamanrasset but in another 50 kilometres away, high in the mountains at an altitude of about 9,000 feet, right in the heart of the country and very favourably situated for making close contact with the Tuaregs, but not for receiving letters as the post doesn't come here. Your letter delighted me with its reassurances about your nephew. I celebrated Easter at Insalah and heard about his accident, but with no details. I hope all trace of it has now gone and that there won't be any after-effects. I shall write to him in a few days and congratulate him on his recovery and send him the medal of the scapular if I've got one light enough, if not the picture. He shouldn't give up his idea of coming here; it isn't very sought after; he would easily get it, and just at this moment he would find very nice superiors, all very decent chaps, and what's more important, he'd find the means of doing a great deal of good among these new populations who only need a little kindness to become friendly...

Br Charles of Jesus

Tamanrasset by Insalah via Biskra-Ouargla,
13 December 1912 *(to Dom Augustin)*[4]

Most Reverend and dearest Father: A letter from the dear good brother Augustin informs me that you have been elected abbot. I pray God with my whole heart to shower graces upon you, to make your time as abbot of Notre

Dame des Neiges a time of holiness for the monastery. May the monastery under your direction be fragrant with the perfume of its virtues, may it be the path to heaven for its monks, and obtain God's glory as much as the most fervent monasteries have ever done.

It would be a great sweetness for me to come and kneel before you and ask for your blessing, but when shall I have this joy? Possibly this summer, but nothing is certain. I am getting older and am in a hurry to do what is possible and useful while there is still time. I would like to show France and our way of life and our Christian families to one of the Tuaregs in my neighbourhood who seems most capable of profiting by such a trip, so I probably won't go back to France except in the company of a Tuareg. Will it be 1913? That's what I would like, but only God knows.

Pray for me, dear Father, pray for all the infidels in the French colonies towards whom Christian France has the same duties as Christian parents towards their children - a thing she seems to overlook...

Br Charles of Jesus

La Renaudie by Bergerac,
8 July 1913 *(to Br Augustin)*

Dearest brother: Thank you for your two excellent letters of 10 March and 24 June. In fact I have been in France for three weeks now with a young Tuareg, a chieftain's son - Muslim but very upright and well-disposed - to whom I am introducing Christianity by its fruits. I would love to come and see you, you know this without my saying it, it would be soothing and profitable to me as it would be to my companion. But I fear it won't be possible; as there are two of us the fares are much more expensive, especially as I am trying to make the trip in every way delightful and edifying for my companion and hence am forced to additional expenditure. This is why I have to restrict my travels and why I don't think we shall be able to pay you a visit. However if it turned out to be possible I would naturally let you know the exact time of our arrival.

I shan't be leaving France before September. Having brought a Tuareg all the way here I am anxious he should spend enough time in France really to profit by his stay. You can write to me until mid-September c/o M. de Blic, Barbiray, par Pont de Pany (Côte d'Or) and afterwards at Insalah...

Br Charles of Jesus

Barbiray by Pont-de-Pany, Côte d'Or,
28 July 1913 *(to Br Augustin)*

Dearest brother: Thank you for your affectionate letter of 22 July and your insistence that we should come and see you. I shall do everything in my power to do this, but cannot absolutely commit myself. The only possible time would be just before embarkation, towards 25 September. I shall come if I can and spend a day with you around that date; I shall write later giving exact details as to the day and time of arrival.

Of course you must know what strength and consolation a visit to Notre Dame des Neiges would give me, but you must also understand the three reasons that give me pause: the extra expense, the fatigue involved for my Tuareg, and the visit having to come at the end of a trip that has already been long for him.

Many thanks for offering to pay half the fare; this isn't necessary as at Marseilles I managed to get a card entitling us to half fares for six months.

Give my very affectionate respects to Fr Abbot and a thousand thanks for his friendly invitation. Ask him to bless me and pray for me...

Br Charles de Foucauld[5]

Tamanrasset by Insalah,
29 November 1913 *(to Br Augustin)*

Dearest brother: May Jesus protect you, grant you a holy

year and a holy life and heaven. I shall pray for you with all my might on Christmas eve, Christmas day and 1 January.

I arrived back at my hermitage 7 days ago and my life has resumed its quiet and regular course. However I think I shall have to spend a short while in France again in 1915. This time I shall certainly visit you, of that you may be sure, and I am already looking forward to it. Meanwhile pray for me and pray for the Tuaregs and all the infidels in the French colonies.

These colonies have extended so much over the past fifteen years that they now contain more than forty million infidels. What is done for their conversion is a drop in the ocean. A few priests are trying to start a fraternity having as goal the involvement of French Christians in the evangelization of their colonies; pray for this fraternity to get established and to work for the glory of God; if such is Jesus's will.[6]

I hope you have good news of your cavalryman in the African service...

Br Charles de Foucauld

Tamanrasset,
26 April 1914 *(to Br Augustin)*

Dearest brother: Many thanks for your good letters of 8 December and 7 March. My letters are few and far between due to excess of work, but my thoughts and my poor prayers are often with you and all my dear fathers and brothers of N.D. des Neiges. Thank them for their pious messages and tell them my heart is with them.

I shan't forget to pray God for your young cousin recently taken from this world, nor for your cavalryman. So good brother François-Regis has gone to join dear Dom Martin and so many other beloved souls who have entered into the light and love of the life of bliss. They are praying for us and helping us to complete our pilgrimage.

I am still hoping to visit you and for a long time in the

summer of 1915, if God so wills; you can well imagine how I look forward to it and how sweet it will be for me to be with you before the tabernacle and to talk about Africa and the kingdom of Jesus in African souls.

My labours in the Tuareg language are not yet finished; I need another five years, probably more, if God grants me life;[7] I am now fifty-five, I'm well, but I'm not as strong as I was.[8] My Tuareg neighbours continue to be very good to me; the process of taming them, of gaining their trust, takes time with races who have been prejudiced against us for so long and are still deeply ignorant.

Goodbye, dearest brother; this is Good Shepherd Sunday. Tell Dom Augustin that I have thought about him today and prayed for him, and ask him to bless me from afar. Commend me to the prayers of all.

Br Charles of Jesus

Tamanrasset,
12 December 1914 (*to Br Augustin*)

Dearest brother: Heartfelt thanks for your welcome letters of 13 September, 20 October, 4 November, and thank you for writing so often in these stormy days. Your letter of the 4th made me very happy through your good news of your cavalryman for whom I hardly dared hope after your letter of 20 October. I had told the bad news to sergeant-major Constant so then hastened to tell him the good. May God be praised for having preserved your nephew and may he also preserve his brother and all the brothers of the fathers and brothers at N.D. des Neiges who are at the front. We must keep very close to each other in this time of anguish. My closest relations on active service, that is to say the sons of my sister and my cousin, are all well so far. General Laperrine was also all right on 16 October. Among friends and less close relations, thirteen have already been killed. Pray for the living and the dead. May God protect France, all the French, all their subjects and their allies! May he bring the good of souls from this ordeal!

You can imagine how much I would like to be with our soldiers, but I think I can be more useful here, helping to preserve peace and calm; our Tuaregs of the Sahara are in any case absolutely calm, totally occupied with their material interests; the entry of Turkey into the lists, to which our people here are utterly indifferent, will do nothing to disturb their calm, I think. The people here would only emerge from it if swept along by a very violent external stimulus, and even then it would be difficult.

So I plan to stay here until the peace, and when peace comes to go for three or four months to France, perhaps five or six. I want to start up a good work, a sort of fraternity for the conversion of the French colonies. At the moment we have fifty million infidels in our colonies: God has given us charge over their souls in putting them under our dominion. Now, when they are shedding their blood with ours, when they are dying so as to defend us, now is surely the moment to remember our duties towards them, of which the first is to try to win their salvation. I shall talk to you about all this at length when peace comes, if God spares me.

Thank you for your news of all our fathers and brothers on active service. Tell them when you write that I pray for them every day with my whole heart.[9]

Ch. de Foucauld

Have the goodness to send this holy picture to your cavalryman. I can't send it direct due to not knowing how to address letters to prisoners. Have you any news of Mgr Bonnet? Is he in good health?

Tamanrasset,
5 February 1915 *(to Br Augustin)*

Dearest brother: Thank you for your letter of 8 December and for your good wishes. Thank you for the news of all our dear fathers and brothers and particularly of those at the front. I hope Fr Germain is better and that all are well.

Oh yes, you can count on a visit of two days, two days at the very least, when peace comes. But when will peace come? Before the summer? That seems to me impossible. In the autumn? Please God, but who knows? What is certain is that it must be a peace that will reduce Germany to impotence for years; otherwise the whole business would start up again before long and in less favourable conditions. All the letters I get from the front are full of confidence in victory, but all say that it will be long.

Here the country is calm. They are not concerned either with the European war or the holy war: they only get worried about things affecting pasturage, the harvest, rain, drought. Despite this calm I think I can be more useful here than elsewhere and I plan to stay here until peace comes. After the peace I shall probably spend some time in France...

Ch. de Foucauld

Tamanrasset by Insalah via Biskra,
15 July 1915 (St Henri) *(to Br Augustin)*

Thank you, dearest brother, for your welcome letter of 25 May which has just arrived, and thank you for the news of the dear fathers and brothers at N.D. des Neiges. God has willed that Br Anastase and Br Ernest should offer the sacrifice of their lives for the salvation of their brothers: they have sacrificed their lives to duty and charity in a matter of moments instead of sacrificing it over a long time in the cloister; they have sacrificed it in the open instead of in the shadow of the convent. Praise be to God who received their sacrifice and will make it a source of grace for France, for their blood-brothers and their brothers in religion; he received them into heaven as good and faithful servants at the very moment when they loved with the greatest love through giving their lives for their neighbour.

Here, absolute calm, as in the whole of French Africa.

My life flows by, externally, in its serenity and regularity. But you can imagine how unquiet my soul is, it hopes for the certainty of victory, the letters I receive from the front are full of confidence; but even the most recent telegrams that arrive are 30 days old, and even the very latest letters and papers are 40 days old (since the war started I've been taking two papers, *l'Echo de Paris* and *La Dépêche algérienne*) so that as I read them I am wondering what has happened since and how matters stand now.

My close relations at the front and at sea are all well. My sister (whom you received at La Bastide) has her three sons in action, one a reserve officer near Soissons, and two naval officers (a sub-lieutenant and a midshipman) in the Mediterranean. God has preserved them up till now; commend them to everyone's prayers. General Laperrine is well...

Ch. de Foucauld

Tamanrasset,
25 September 1915 *(to Br Augustin)*

Thank you, dearest brother, for your letter of 16 July and your card of the 22nd; God is truly testing you, my poor one, and testing all your dear ones by the sudden and tragic death of your brother-in-law. My prayers join with yours for him and for those he leaves behind, especially for your cavalryman for whom it is hard indeed to be so far away at a moment like this; in praying for them I am praying for you who are sharing their suffering. Peace to men of good will: this phrase which came down from heaven on the first day of the Christian era is the sweet promise of eternal happiness for your dear departed. And if his soul bore some traces of earthly dust, then the prayers of his relations and of N.D. des Neiges will have quickly brushed them away.

Here, deep calm. Things aren't going well for the Italians in Tripolitania. They are paying dear for their inexperience. But the disturbances have not crossed the frontier; this is anyway well guarded by our troops. Good news of General Laperrine and of my close relations... I weep with you for Br Ernest. God has welcomed him into heaven among the martyrs of charity. This war isn't like other wars. Those who die in it give their lives to save their brothers and sisters not only from degrading subjugation but from every kind of cruelty, every kind of violence, every kind of most inhuman infamy. They are truly martyrs for love of neighbour.

Thank you for your news of all our fathers and brothers under arms; you can imagine how I pray for them, asking God to look after them and help them to do good; they are missionaries among our soldiers, perhaps not by word but by example, virtue and goodness which have greater value. God brings good out of evil. Laws made against religion have the effect of spreading religion; a war that covers the world in blood and dereliction brings souls back to God and teaches Europe a necessary and I hope a fruitful lesson...

Ch. de F.

Tamanrasset,
11 April 1916 *(to Br Augustin)*

Dearest brother: Thank you for your welcome letter of 5 January. May God look after you and look after all the fathers and brothers of Notre-Dame des Neiges, those at the front and those in the cloister; may he look after your poor prisoner and his family, and may he protect France.

Our Tuaregs remain calm despite the capture of Djanet by the Senoussists and the revolt of some Loullemiden near the Niger, not a very serious one, they say.

My thoughts and prayers are with you. Tell your poor prisoner that I'm praying for him. I embrace you with my whole heart as I love you in the heart of Jesus.

Ch. de F.

This is the last letter addressed by Charles de Foucauld

to any of his Trappist brothers. But the archives at Notre-Dame des Neiges contain three hitherto unpublished letters from his sister after his assassination in December 1916 - two to Dom Augustin, the abbot, and one to Brother Augustin:

Grasse, Villa Fragonard,
7 January 1917 *(to Dom Augustin)*

Reverend Father: The deep affection that you have always felt for my brother, Father de Foucauld, compels me to let you know the tragic news that has reached us. The Rev. Assistant General of the White Fathers has written to tell us that he was killed on 13 December, at Tamanrasset, together with three soldiers who were with him, by a raiding party of thirty horsemen who then disappeared. The commanding officer of the Oasis Sahariennes to whom we telegraphed speaks of a raiding party of Ajjers. We are deeply grieved by this tragic loss, but we have the consolation of telling ourselves that my brother gave his life for the faith and for France, and that such an end worthily crowns a life totally consecrated to God and his country.

My brother died ten days after our youngest son who also met a tragic death. He was sub-lieutenant on the 'Surprise', torpedoed by the Germans at Foumchal. I thank God he was still pious and must have been prepared for anything that happened; nevertheless we would be very grateful to you if in your prayers you would unite the memory of the nephew with that of the uncle. May God's will be done, and always loved, even when it brings the cross.

I hope that our two dear victims may even now be reunited in heaven.

Would you have the kindness, Reverend Father, to impart the news of my brother's death to Monsignor the Bishop of Viviers in whose diocese he was ordained. I do not know whether Mgr Bonnet is still there, who honoured my brother with such generous sympathy.

M. de Blic joins with me, Reverend Father, in begging you to accept the expression of our deepest respect.

Foucauld de Blic

Grasse, Villa Fragonard,
4 February 1917 *(to Dom Augustin)*

Reverend Father: We have now received detailed accounts of the last moments of my brother, Father Charles of Jesus; your affection for him, to which your excellent letter of 10 January bears witness, encourages me to write to let you know the circumstances that accompanied his end.

It was not, as we previously thought, on 13 December that he met a glorious death but on 1 December (which in 1916 fell on the first Friday of the month, the day consecrated to the Sacred Heart so ardently loved by my brother). Towards 7 o'clock in the evening about 50 pillagers from the Ajjers arrived at Tamanrasset; one of them entered his room telling him he was bringing letters from Tarhaouhaout; he seized him and, with the help of a few other men, overpowered him. The bandits also killed two Saharians who were visiting my brother; as for him he was shot down at point blank by a bullet beneath his ear. A third Saharian, who had come to bring the mail, was also assassinated. The four crimes were committed by raiders helped, alas, by a few natives of the Hoggar.

My poor brother's body and those of the other three victims were totally stripped of their clothes by the pillagers. They were buried through the good offices of a former servant of the Father and a few natives.

We have received several accounts of these tragic events. In one of them (sent on 9 January by Captain Depommier of Insalah) it was said that the assassins wanted to compel the Father to say a Muslim prayer and when he refused one of them shot him from behind the head killing him outright. The Captain, who loved my brother and had known him for eight years, says he could not help smiling at this death, such an ideal one for him! It is in fact martyrdom bringing to a worthy end Fr Charles of Jesus's life of sacrifice. What a consolation for us and what an example to our children! Please accept, Reverend Father, the expression of my deepest respect.

Foucauld de Blic

P.S. We do not yet know what has become of my brother's manuscripts.

Grasse, Villa Fragonard,
24 November 1917 *(to Br Augustin)*

Good brother: Today I have received a letter from Rev. Fr Voillard of the White Fathers: the pectoral cross belonging to Dom Martin, the late abbot of Notre Dame des Neiges, is certainly among the pious objects found at Tamanrasset; the White Fathers will send it to Rev. Fr Abbot as soon as the war is over and transport by sea runs less risk of being torpedoed. They will send it forthwith if the Rev. Fr Abbot so wishes, but I think it would be more prudent to wait till the end of the war.

I thank you, good brother, for sending me this letter of my brother's which I return along with the pictures you ask for; not many are left, so I cannot send more than these.

Please believe my respectful feelings, good brother,

M. de Blic

As Brother Augustin has figured largely in this section, it should be noted that he lived to the ripe age of 80 and died at Notre-Dame des Neiges in 1941. As for Notre-Dame des Neiges itself, it is still a flourishing monastery and now has an extended guest-house where hundreds of priests and lay people go every year for the spiritual exercises.

Charles de Foucauld's followers now

Charles de Foucauld had no followers in his lifetime, but what is called 'The Family of Brother Charles' has come into being since his death. It consists of:

(1) The Little Brothers of Jesus, started by Fr Voillaume and four young priests in 1932 in Algeria. There are now well over 250 Brothers in over fifty 'fraternities' (i.e., small groups living according to the principles of poverty, hospitality, and adoration of the blessed Sacrament - whether in the desert proper or in the wilderness of the urban centres) in 25 different countries;

(2) The Little Sisters of Jesus, founded at Touggourt in the Sahara in 1939 by Little Sister Magdaleine of Jesus, and now numbering over 1,100 sisters in 200 'fraternities' of 50 different nationalities and based on the same principles as those of the Little Brothers;

(3) The Union of Priests founded in 1952 - priests doing their own thing as diocesan priests but given fresh inspiration by Charles de Foucauld's life;

(4) The Jesus/Caritaas fraternity started in 1954 by Fr Voillaume; a wide-ranging group of men and women who devote themselves in a context of poverty, chastity and obedience (though without necessarily becoming religious, priests or nuns) to Charles de Foucauld's principles of living, rather than preaching, the presence of Christ in the world: 'Your vocation is to shout the gospel from the rooftops, not in words, but with your life';

(5) The Charles of Jesus Secular Fraternity. This is really wide-ranging – priests, single people, married people may belong – the aim being total hospitality and availability to everyone who comes, combined with adoration of the blessed Sacrament without which everything else would be 'as dry as dust'.

Such is the 'Brother Charles of Jesus Family' which is rapidly developing in all parts of the world.

Notes

Chapter I

[1] Contrary to Charles de Foucauld's usage, the initial letter of pronouns relating to God has not been given a capital in this translation except when needed for clarification. Other initial capitals have also been dropped in accordance with present-day practice.

[2] Charles de Foucauld had already visited this Trappist monastery in Syria on his travels and been greatly drawn to it.

Chapter II

[1] Dom Polycarpe was sub-prior at Akbès from 1882 until his death and also novice-master at the time of Charles de Foucauld's arrival. Let it be said here that the prefixes of Most or Very Reverend preceding Father or Dom have often been omitted in this translation in the interests of greater simplification.

[2] This was Charles de Foucauld's cousin from whom, and from whose family, it had manifestly been a great wrench to part. All his references to his nearest and dearest refer to her and her family as well as to his sister and hers.

[3] Presumably Jesus Mary Joseph Blessed.

[4] To write every two months.

[5] Dom Martin had advised this work for Br Albéric.

[6] At this time Trappist abbots and priors were having a series of meetings in Rome (the cause of Dom Martin's postponements of his visit to Akbès) in an effort to find a way of uniting the different observances that had grown up within the Order. Charles de Foucauld feared that unification would lead to mitigation of some of the strict elements in the Rule that had drawn him to the Order in the first place.

[7] A short-lived foundation of N.D. des Neiges in the department of Gard.

[8] Not, of course, to be confused with the prior, the great Dom Louis de Gonzague.

[9] Dom Louis de Gonzague, prior of N.D. du Sacré-Coeur, wrote to his brother, Dom Martin, on the same subject:'For a fortnight now the barometer has been between 40 and 46 by day, we've never had such a hot summer; little Fr Louis has been ill with it, but he's better now that the nights are cooler. Fr Marie Albéric has been a most attentive nurse to him; thus they have both missed two weeks of theology but will, I hope, return to it with renewed enthusiasm'.

[10] Thus lightly does Charles de Foucauld refer to a period of illness that caused his superiors some anxiety.

Chapter III

[1] In his letters Charles de Foucauld had the habit of totally capitalizing the words 'Jesus' and 'heart' (*coeur*). These capitals have been dropped in the translation.

[2] Dom Louis de Gonzague, abbot of Staouéli. This account of Charles de Foucauld's new orientation is of great interest as in no other existing letter to his Trappist brothers is it given.

Chapter IV

[1] This is perhaps the place to say how frequently Charles de Foucauld underlines for emphasis in his letters to Fr Jérôme. This page in the French edition is rich with italics. In the English translation these have not been reproduced.

[2] Having been out of touch for so long with N.D. des Neiges Charles de Foucauld did not know that Fr Geniez had died on 19 March 1898.

[3] An allusion to St Bernard's brother, Gérard.

[4] Fr Polycarpe had died in 1895, aged 68.

Chapter V

[1] Fr Jérôme had been back at Staouéli for a long time now and Fr Henri had become its prior.

Chapter VI

[1] The Apostolic Prefect for the Sahara.

[2] Charles de Foucauld made a brief pilgrimage to Sainte-Baume (where there is a shrine to St Mary Magdalen) between leaving N.D. des Neiges and embarking for Algiers.

[3] Omission-dots occurring at the end of letters stand in for the valedictory phrases that the reader now knows well and can fill in for himself.

[23] This would refer to the anti-clerical laws in force in France at this time.

[4] It is already becoming clear that Br Augustin is the companion that Charles de Foucauld would have liked to have if Dom Martin would agree. He was certainly one of the 'one or two' mentioned in the letter to Henry de Castries.

[5] Father General of the White Fathers.

[6] Fr Jérôme's baptismal name was also Charles.

[7] It was the custom that when a member of a Trappist community died, each priest celebrated three masses for the repose of his soul. The fact that Charles de Foucauld did so shows how close he felt his bonds with the community to be.

[8] Obviously a reference to himself.

[9] This was the year when the future of the monastery at Akbès came under discussion.

Chapter VII

[1] It was with the Tuareg tribes of the south of the Sahara that he henceforth felt his mission to be.

[2] The new abbot was called Dom Martin II and came from the monastery at Aiguebelle somewhat against his will.

[3] A monk at N.D. des Neiges who had written to Charles de Foucauld asking for an account of his life and aims so that he might have something to show any interested priest. Charles de Foucauld took great trouble with this letter and kept a copy.

[4] The new abbot of N.D. des Neiges, Dom Martin II, having retired after three years. Dom Augustin had been ordained priest at Viviers with Charles de Foucauld.

[5] No explanation is given as to why Charles de Foucauld from now henceforward (with one exception) signs himself in this new way.

[6] This fraternity had already been adumbrated, for Mgr Bonnet had approved its principles when Charles de Foucauld went to see him in early March 1909.

[7] Charles de Foucauld was engaged on a Tuareg-French dictionary and had already translated the gospels into Tuareg.

[8] As Charles de Foucauld has often expressed a wish to die in the course of these letters, the following extract from a letter to his cousin, Madame de Bondy, written about this time, needs to be quoted: 'I cannot say that I wish for death; I wished for it once; now I see so much good to be done, so many souls without a shepherd'.

[9] N.D. des Neiges lost seven of its religious on active service.

Index

A

B

C

D

E

F

G

H

I

J

L

M

N

O

P

R

S

T

V

W

X

Other writings of Charles de Foucauld from Orbis . . .

Silent Pilgrimage to God

The Spirituality of Charles de Foucauld

edited by a Little Brother of Jesus

preface by René Voillaume

Paper $3.95

"The brilliant, virile spirituality of Father Charles de Foucauld is highlighted in an anonymously edited book called *Silent Pilgrimage to God.* The facts of his life are fairly well known today: his career in the French military, his rediscovery of God, his life as a Cistercian in the Holy Land and then the final years as a hermit in the Sahara. He died without a convert or a disciple, yet today, the Little Brothers of Jesus and the Little Sisters of Jesus are flourishing. What de Foucauld sowed and what God has blessed was the fruit of his meditation and his love for the Eucharist. . . . The book is so good that one is tempted to keep on quoting. Instead, treat yourself and your parish library to copies of *Silent Pilgrimage to God.*" ***The Priest***

" 'My vocation is to shout the Gospel from the rooftops, not in words, but with my life.' With this theme as the guiding force of his life and with unswerving dedication to his vocation, Charles de Foucauld embarked on a pilgrimage to bring Christianity to all people. Modest, self-effacing and devoted to spreading the Gospel, de Foucauld has today emerged as a major spiritual writer and one of the most fascinating of modern mystics, an almost legendary figure. This book outlines the characteristic features of de Foucauld's faith, discusses some of his insights and presents a particularly fine selection of texts that are typical of his single mindedness in the service of God."

New Book Review

Other Orbis books by followers of Charles de Foucauld . . .

By Arturo Paoli . . .

Freedom to Be Free

Paper $4.95

"Based largely upon biblical sources and upon the need of the third world to advance beyond the state of oppression, this book concentrates on liberation, but with perspectives which differ from the majority of the present-day theologies of liberation. It sees life as a 'journey toward freedom, because freedom is the permanent part of history.' Leaving to others the social, economic, and political dimensions of liberation, Paoli focuses upon its spirituality. His book is more of a dialogue with the reader than a systematic presentation." ***Cross and Crown***

"This book is full of eye-opening reflections on how Jesus liberated man through poverty, the Cross, the Eucharist and prayer. Because he stressed both contemplation and community action in the pursuit of freedom, Paoli's book deserves wide distribution and reading, here and everywhere." ***America***

"The chapter on the Eucharist is worth the price of this thrilling book. There is so much in this book, in every chapter, that deserves and will receive the rapt attention of students of the Gospel, which will richly reward real study and re-reading again and again. Prayer, Mary, the Eucharist, grace—here is the Gospel in depth." ***The Living Church***

Meditations on Saint Luke

Paper $4.95
Cloth $8.95

"The author lets old texts reinvigorate themselves in his whole being. His illustrations, taken from our day and related to deep experience, should help anyone understand Luke's gospel better. Meditations like these will help keep Bible study from becoming a mere fad."

The New Review of Books and Religion

"If you are ready to take the time to disagree and agree both profoundly, then this will prove an extremely fruitful book of meditation in the light of liberation theology.

"Be prepared for some magnificent pages on topics such as chastity, freedom and Mary.

"Be prepared as well for some deep-rooted challenges to a great many things you and I have taken for granted for too long.

"But mostly, be prepared to let your mind float with Paoli's and you will be challenged to reflect deeply upon your faith and, perhaps, to pursue spiritual depths within yourself that would otherwise remain sedated."

Western Catholic Reporter

ARTURO PAOLI was ordained in 1940 and has served as a seminary professor, director of Italian Catholic Action, and chaplain on ships taking immigrants to South America. In 1955 he entered the Congregation of the Little Brothers, and in 1959 launched their first community in South America at Fortin Olmos in Argentina, where his service to the poor and the young has brought him into frequent confrontations with civil authorities.

By Carlo Carretto . . .

The God Who Comes

Cloth $4.95

"His reflections are tremendous; that's the only word strong enough to describe them." ***The Priest***

Love Is for Living

Cloth $6.95; Paper $4.95

"Don't buy this book to read; if you buy it, taste it, sip it, relish it, delight in it. Make it an evening retreat. Think what it is saying and then you'll get your money's worth. Fact is, it just might change your life so that money wouldn't matter nearly so much as it does now."

The Western Michigan Catholic

Summoned by Love

Cloth $7.95; Paper $4.95

"*Summoned by Love* is a wonderful book. I hope you come to own a copy rather than beg, borrow, or steal it (metaphorically speaking), because, if you are anything like this particular reader, you will want to read it many times over and underline a cumulative third of its contents. People ask me whether I actually read all the books I review. Well, friends and neighbors, I was vitalized enough on this one to have gone through *Summoned by Love* some five or six times."

Church World

CARLO CARRETTO is one of the Little Brothers of Jesus. He divides his time between the order's house in the Sahara and Spello (near Assisi) in the Umbrian hills, where he lives the life of a hermit.